Thinking Theory
PREP BOOK
Written by Nicola Cantan

www.colourfulkeys.ie

© 2016 Colorful Keys. All Rights Reserved.

WARNING! The contents of this publication are protected by copyright law.
To copy or reproduce them by any method is an infringement of the copyright law.

What is Thinking Theory?

→ Thinking Theory is a series of music theory workbooks designed to accelerate learning while providing plenty of reinforcement of each concept.

→ All concepts are presented in a clear and concise way and page layouts are clean and consistent.

→ No topic is introduced without being revisited several times later in the book.

→ Thinking Theory is designed so you can start anywhere in the series. Concepts are not left out of later books, just covered more quickly.

→ The flashcard games provide a unique way to learn away from the page, and make learning and teaching more secure and more fun.

→ The "Level Up!" tests at the end of each chapter and book, allow you to evaluate student learning and plan their next step.

→ The Thinking Theory Plus books provide a lateral move for students who have finished one book but are not quite ready for the next.

→ Singing with solfa (movable do) is integrated into the theory books. Solfa helps students with ear training, transposing, sight reading and composition.

Concepts covered in this book...

→ Music alphabet

→ Piano key names

→ Intervals: step & skip/2nd & 3rd

→ Note values: quarter note, half note, dotted half note & whole note

→ Rest values: quarter rest, half rest & whole rest

→ Time signatures: $\frac{2}{4}$ $\frac{3}{4}$ $\frac{4}{4}$

→ Landmark notes: bass C, bass F, middle C, treble G & treble C

→ Dynamics: piano & forte

→ Solfa: do, re & mi

→ Scales: C major

Contents

New concept pages are shown in bold.

Chapter 1	**Music Alphabet** 1		Chapter 4	Note naming 22
	Piano Keys 2			**C major scale** 23
	Steps and skips in the alphabet 3			Note naming 24
	Quarter notes and half notes 4			Note naming 25
	4:4 time signature 5			**Solfa: mi** 26
	Rhythms in 4:4 6			Note naming with keys 27
	Level Up! Chapter 1 Test 7			Level Up! Chapter 4 Test 28
Chapter 2	**Dotted half notes and whole notes** 8		Chapter 5	Solfa 29
	2:4 and 3:4 time signatures 9			Intervals 30
	Patterns on the staff 10			C scale 31
	Bass F, Middle C, Treble G 11			Terms 32
	Note naming 12			Rhythm 33
	Piano and forte 13			Note drawing 34
	Level Up! Chapter 2 Test 14			Level Up! Chapter 5 Test 35
Chapter 3	**Quarter, half and whole rests** 15		Chapter 6	Level Up! The Final Test 36
	Rhythms 16			Level Up! The Final Test 37
	Intervals: 2nd and 3rd 17			Level Up! The Final Test 38
	Solfa: do and re 18			
	Bass C and Treble C 19			
	Note naming 20			
	Level Up! Chapter 3 Test 21			

About Nicola Cantan

Nicola Cantan began teaching piano in 2004, and has always strived to find new ways to engage students in learning. She uses games, improvisation and composing to accelerate her students' progress at the piano and broaden their musical knowledge.

Nicola wrote the 'Thinking Theory' books when she saw the struggle some of her students were having preparing for theory examinations. She wanted a book that regularly reinforced concepts in a systematic way, with a clean layout and clear explanations. Thus 'Thinking Theory' was born.

FLASHCARD GAMES

All the flashcard games can be played with the corresponding Thinking Theory Flashcards which can be downloaded at www.colourfulkeys.ie/thinking-theory.

To play these games, the cards will need to printed one-sided, with the answer on a separate card. You may want to print two sets, one to be used as regular flashcards (printed back to back) and one to be used for games (printed on one side).

You can play these games with the flashcards for one or more chapters at a time, or with the complete set for the whole book. Games like this are a fantastic way to reinforce learning off the page, and allow drilling of concepts in a fun way. Try to revisit each flashcard set periodically by playing a different game, to foster long term and reliable memory.

MEMORY

1. This is a game for one or more players.
2. Lay out all the cards face down.
3. Turn over two cards at a time. If they match, put those cards aside. If they don't match, turn them back over.
4. Keep going until all cards have been matched.

(This game can also be played with multiple players taking turns.)

MATCH

1. This is a game for one player.
2. Layout all the term cards face-up on the floor.
3. See how fast you can match the answer cards, by placing each card on top of the term that matches.
4. Time yourself and try to beat your time on the next go!

PAIRS

1. This is a game for two or more players.
2. Shuffle the cards and deal 4 to each player. Place the remainder of the cards in a pile between the players..
3. Each player takes turns to draw one card from the pile in the centre.
4. If s/he has a matching pair, s/he should place it face up beside them.
5. The winner is the one with the most pairs when all the cards have been drawn.

© Copyright 2016 Colourful Keys

SNAP

1. This is a game for two players.
2. Shuffle the cards and divide into two equal piles, one for each player.
3. On the count of three both players turn over the top card from her/his pile.
4. If the cards match, either player can shout "SNAP!".
5. The first player to say "SNAP!" wins all of the turned over cards, and adds them to her/his pile.
6. The winner is the first to win all the other cards, or the one with the most cards when time is up.

GO FISH!

1. This is a game for two or more players.
2. Shuffle the cards and deal 5 to each player. Place the remainder of the cards in a pile between the players..
3. Each player takes turns to ask another player for cards that would match one of her/his own. For example "Got any E's?" or "Got a crescendo?".
4. The player can continue asking for more cards until the other player does not have the card they need, and tells them to "Go fish!".
5. If told to "Go fish!" the player should pick up a card from the centre pile.
6. As pairs are found, they should be placed face down in front of them.
7. The winner is the first to get rid of all her/his cards. If two players do this at the same time, the winner is the one with the most pairs.

CUCKOO

1. This is a game for two or more players.
2. Remove one card from the deck and place it aside.
3. Shuffle the cards and deal all the cards between the players. It's OK if some players may get more cards than others.
4. Each player should sort through the cards and put down any pairs s/he finds, without letting the other players see her/his cards.
5. One player at a time offers her/his cards (face down) to the player to her/his left.
6. The player to the left takes one card from her/his hand.
7. If this makes a pair, the player to the left puts the pair down beside her/him.
8. Continue like this until all the pairs have been found. The player left with the "Cuckoo" is the loser.

✏️ Fill in the missing letters. Be careful, some are going backwards!

A ___ C ___ E ___ G

___ B ___ D ___ F ___

B ___ D ___ F ___ A

G F ___ D ___ B ___

E D C ___ A ___ F

F G ___ B ___ D ___

Chapter 1

✏️ Circle the correct letter underneath each keyboard.

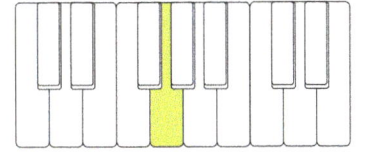

A B C D E F G

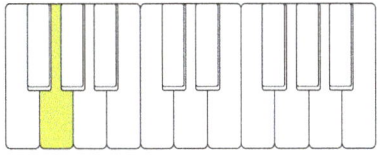

A B C D E F G

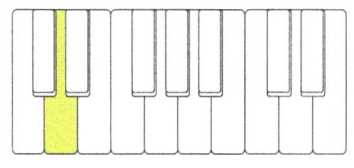

A B C D E F G

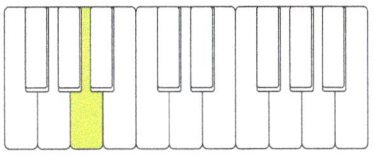

A B C D E F G

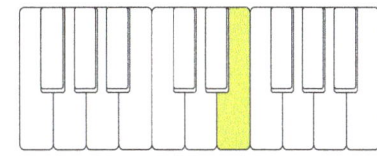

A B C D E F G

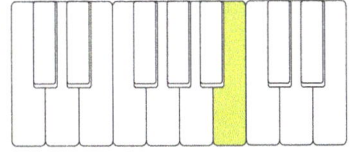

A B C D E F G

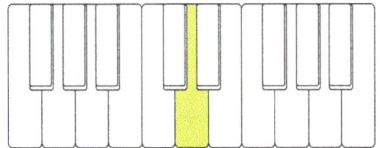

A B C D E F G

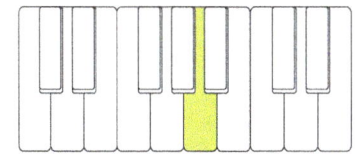

A B C D E F G

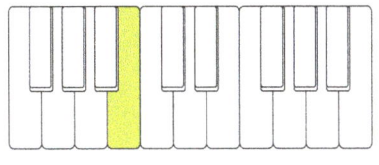

A B C D E F G

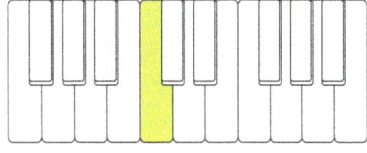

A B C D E F G

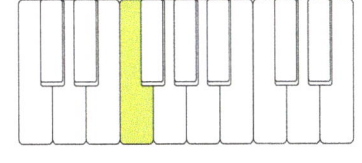

A B C D E F G

A B C D E F G

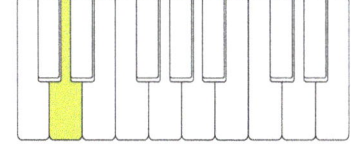

A B C D E F G

Chapter 1 — Thinking Theory Prep Book

> ➤ A step is the distance between two notes beside each other on the keyboard, e.g. A & B.
> ➤ A skip is the distance between two notes which are one note apart, e.g. A & C.

✏️ Circle either step or skip below each of these pairs.

A B	**B D**	**C E**	**F G**
STEP or SKIP	STEP or SKIP	STEP or SKIP	STEP or SKIP

G F	**F D**	**C A**
STEP or SKIP	STEP or SKIP	STEP or SKIP

B G	**A F**	**A G**	**E D**
STEP or SKIP	STEP or SKIP	STEP or SKIP	STEP or SKIP

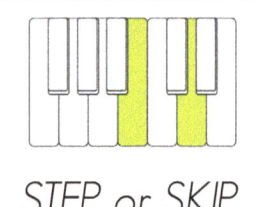 STEP or SKIP  STEP or SKIP  STEP or SKIP

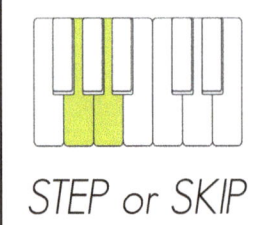 STEP or SKIP 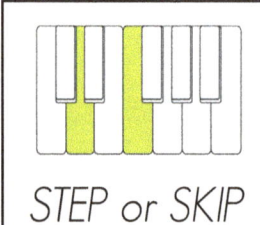 STEP or SKIP  STEP or SKIP 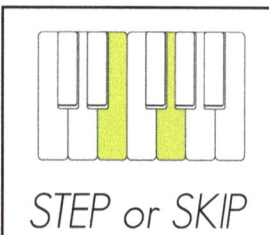 STEP or SKIP

Thinking Theory Prep Book — Chapter 1

New Ingredients: Note Values

♩ = quarter note = 1 beat

𝅗𝅥 = half note = 2 beats

✏️ Practice drawing the new ingredients.

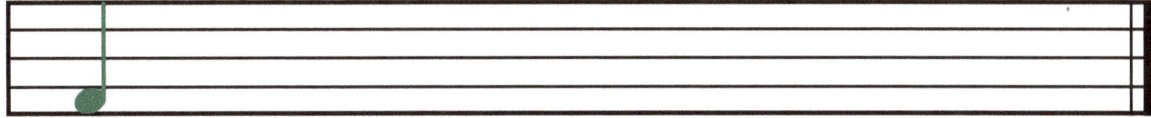

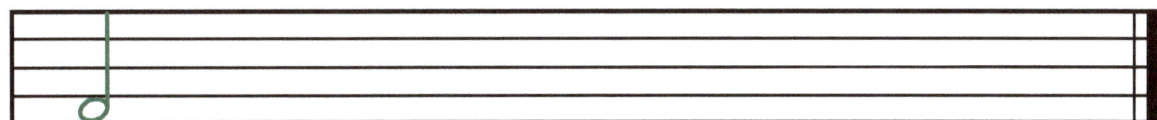

✏️ Circle the matching number of beats for each group of fruit.

   ♩ + ♩   𝅗𝅥 + ♩   ♩ + 𝅗𝅥 + ♩

   𝅗𝅥   𝅗𝅥 + ♩   𝅗𝅥

   ♩ + ♩   𝅗𝅥 + 𝅗𝅥 + ♩   𝅗𝅥 + 𝅗𝅥

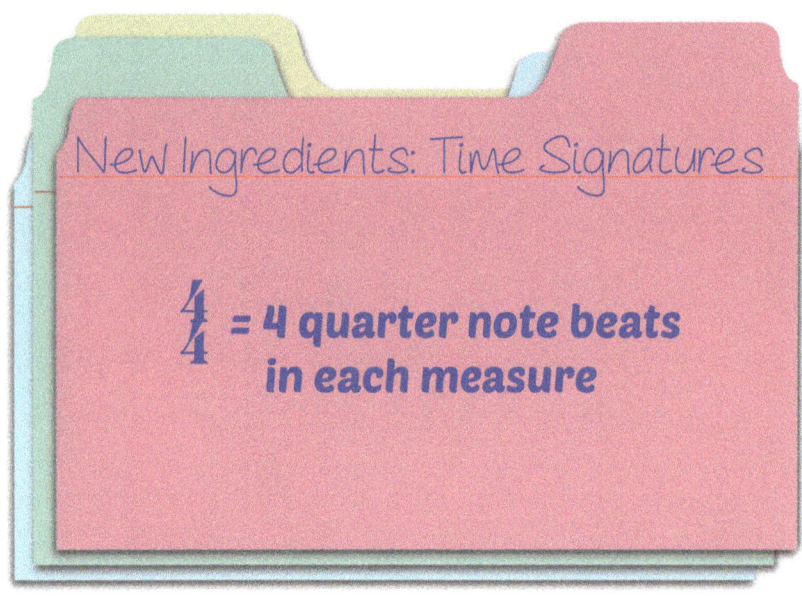

✏️ Put an 'X' through any measures which are incorrect.

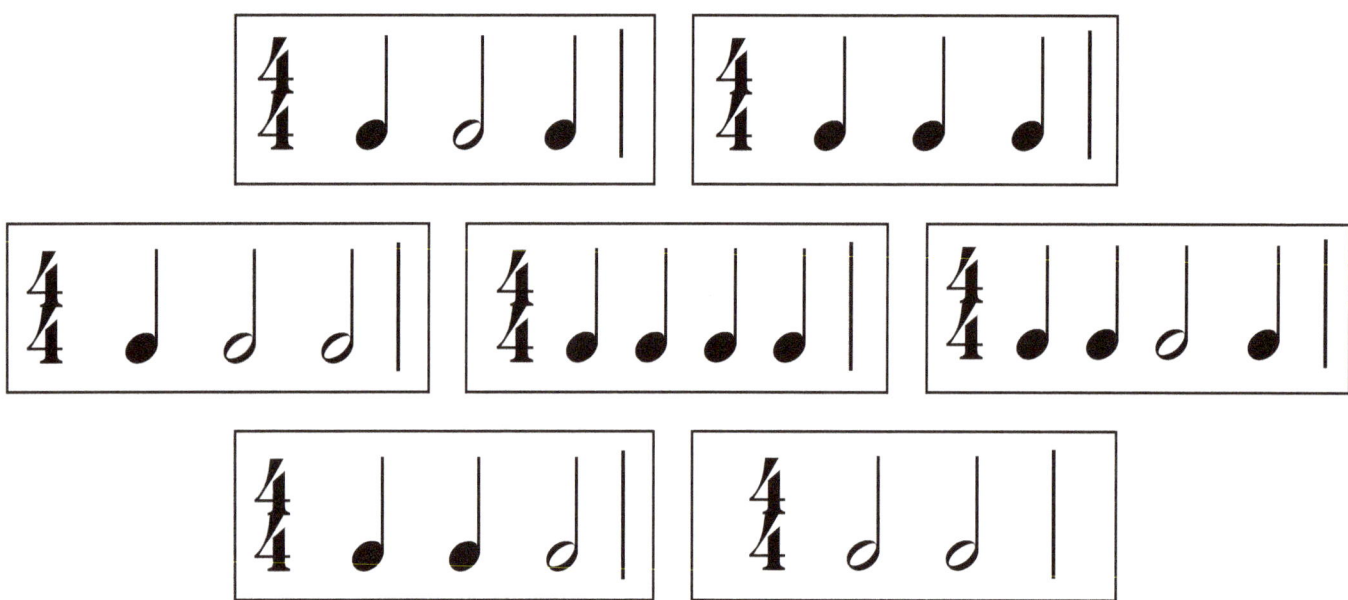

✏️ Compose your own rhythms using a mix of quarter notes & half notes.

Practice clapping these rhythms while counting.

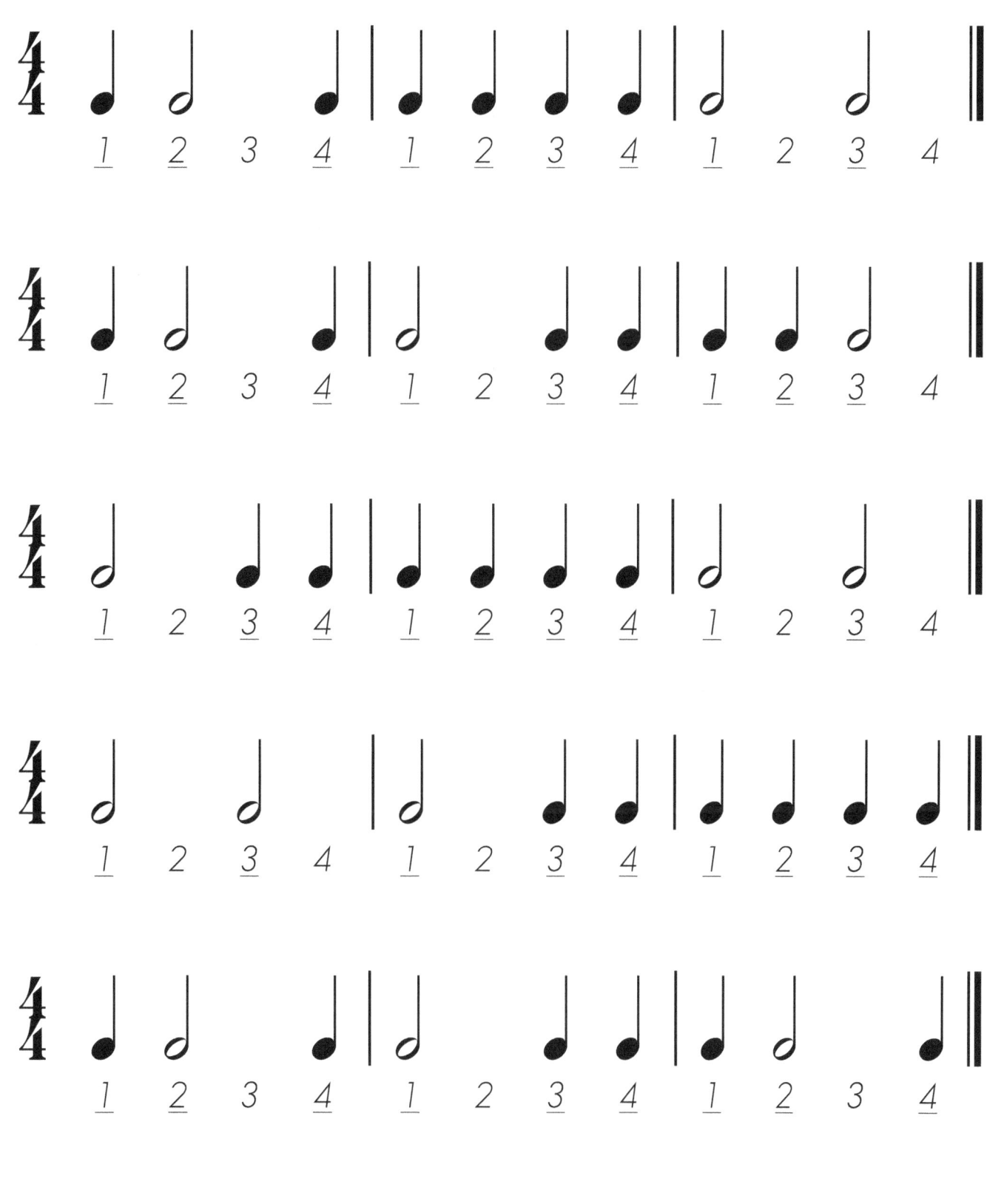

Chapter 1 Thinking Theory Prep Book

Level Up!
Get ready for chapter 2 by answering these questions (without looking back through your book!)

1. Write the letter name under each highlighted key.

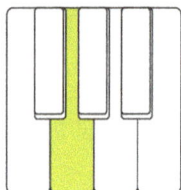 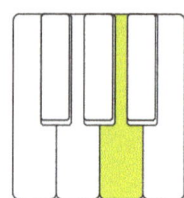 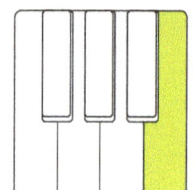 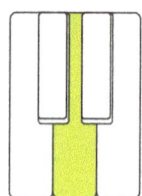 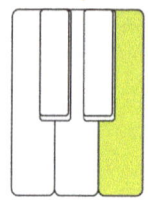

____   ____   ____   ____   ____

2. Fill in the blanks in the music alphabet.

B ___ D ___ F ___ A ___ C

3. Are these pairs steps or skips?

| **B C** | **D F** | **G A** | **E C** |
| STEP or SKIP | STEP or SKIP | STEP or SKIP | STEP or SKIP |

4. Fill in the missing note values to complete the measures.

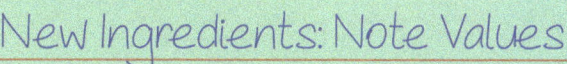

New Ingredients: Note Values

𝅗𝅥. = dotted half note = 3 beats

𝅝 = whole note = 4 beats

✏️ Practice drawing the new ingredients.

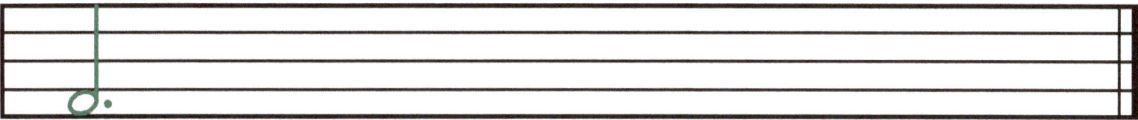

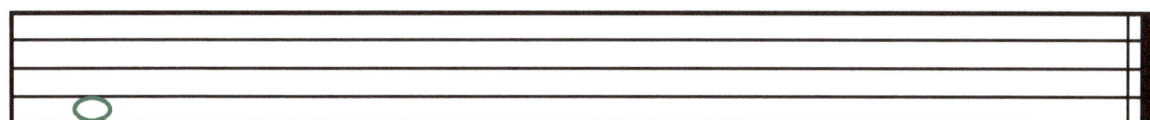

✏️ Circle the matching number of beats for each group of fruit.

   𝅝 + 𝅗𝅥.   𝅗𝅥 + 𝅗𝅥.   𝅝 + ♩ + ♩

   𝅗𝅥. + 𝅗𝅥.   𝅝 + 𝅗𝅥 + ♩   𝅗𝅥 + 𝅗𝅥.

   𝅗𝅥 + 𝅗𝅥.   𝅗𝅥 + 𝅝   𝅗𝅥 + ♩ + ♩

New Ingredients: Time Signatures

$\frac{2}{4}$ = 2 quarter note beats in each measure

$\frac{3}{4}$ = 3 quarter note beats in each measure

✏️ Put an 'X' through any measures which are incorrect.

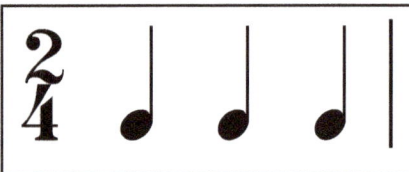
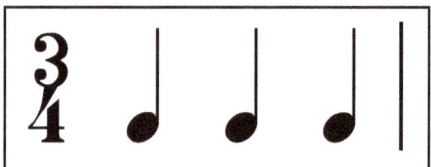

✏️ Compose your own rhythms using a mixture of note values.

$\frac{2}{4}$

$\frac{3}{4}$

Circle either line or space below each of these notes.

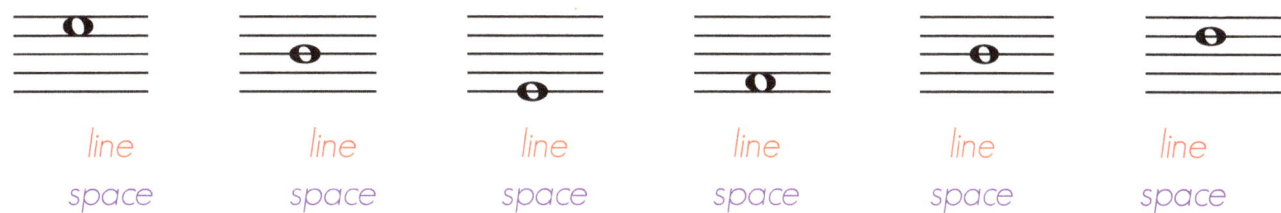

 Circle either up or down below each of these pairs.

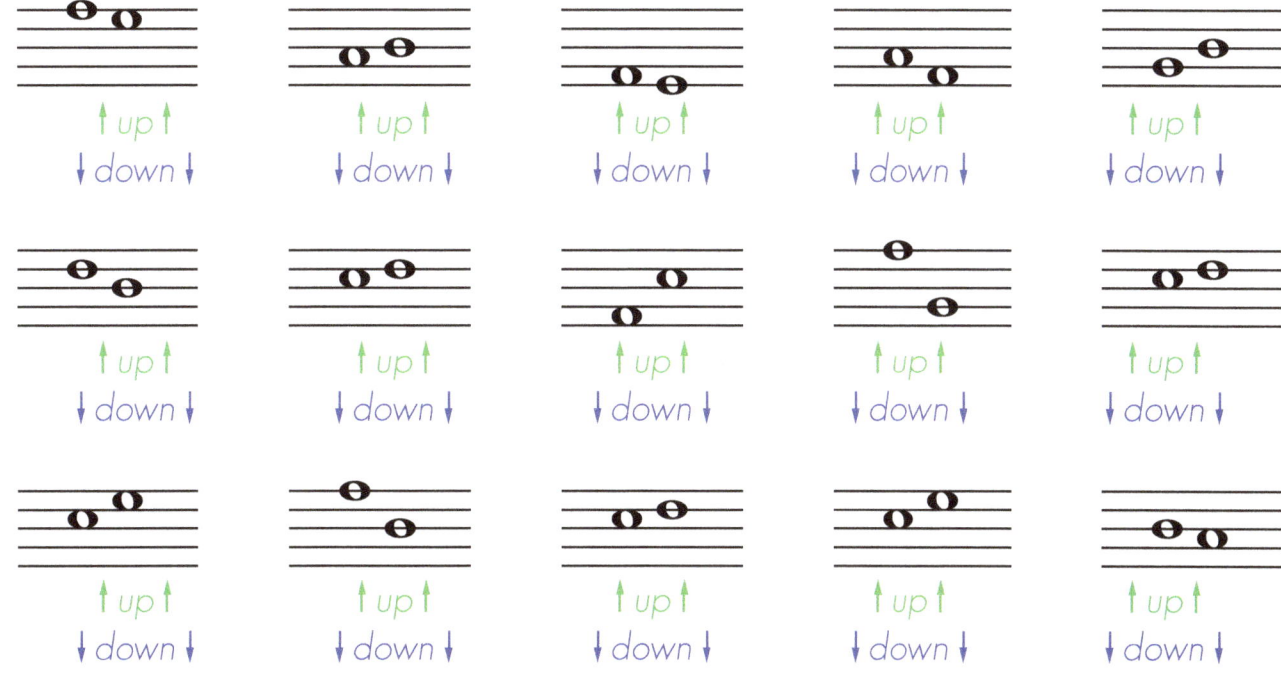

 Circle either step or skip below each of these pairs.

Chapter 2

New Ingredients: Landmark Notes

Bass F **Middle C** **Treble G**

✏️ Practice drawing the new ingredients.

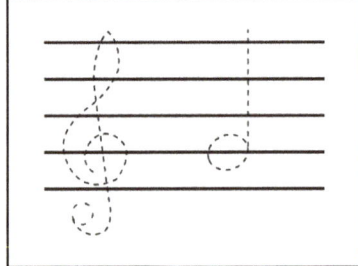 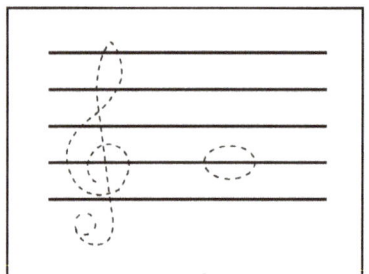 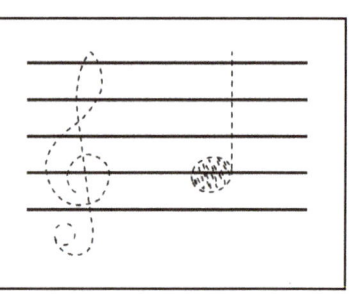

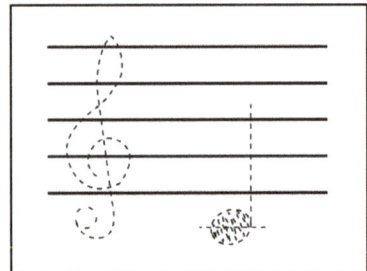 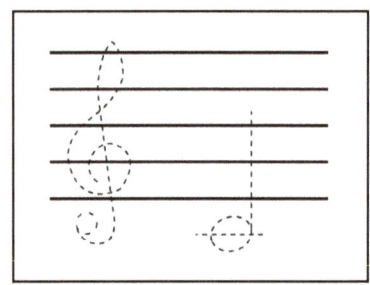 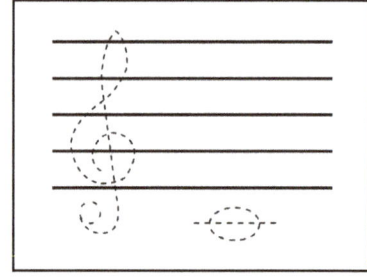

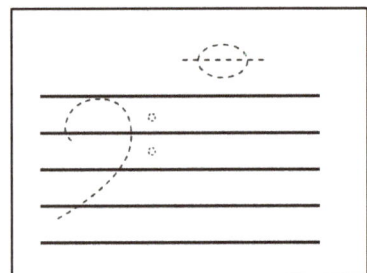 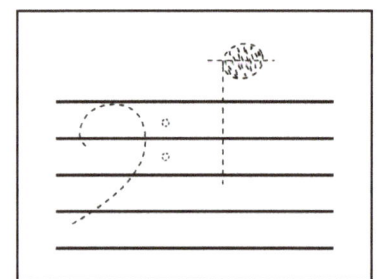 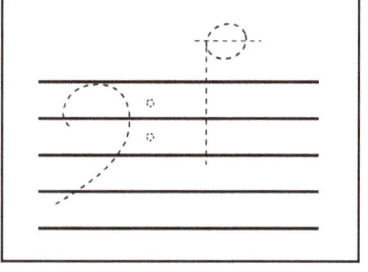

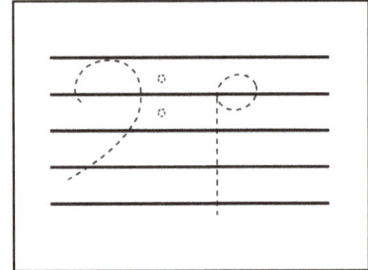 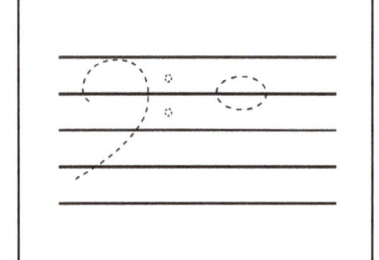 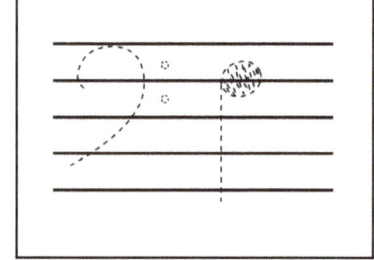

Thinking Theory Prep Book — Chapter 2

 Circle the matching fruit for each note.

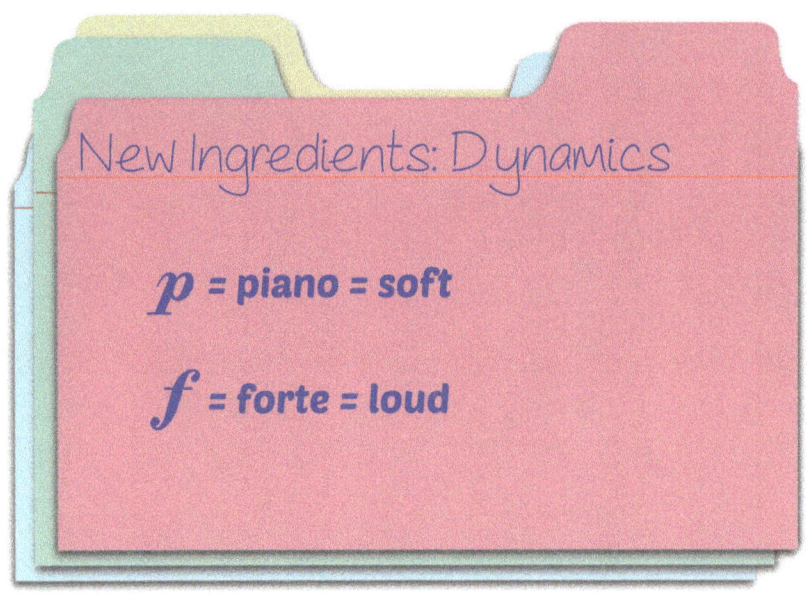

New Ingredients: Dynamics

p = piano = soft

f = forte = loud

✏️ Are these animals loud or soft?

OWL	LION	PIG
f or p	f or p	f or p

DOG	MOUSE	HIPPO
f or p	f or p	f or p

Level Up!
Get ready for chapter 3 by answering these questions (without looking back through your book!)

1. Write the letter name under each note.

_____   _____   _____   _____

2. Circle step or skip below these pairs of notes.

step　　　step　　　step　　　step　　　step
skip　　　skip　　　skip　　　skip　　　skip

3. Match the symbol with its full name.

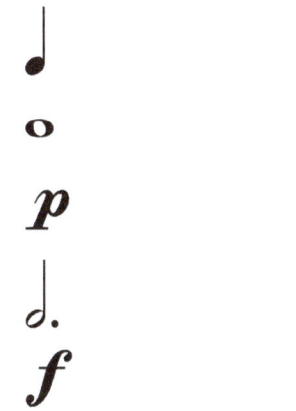

piano

forte

dotted half note

whole note

quarter note

4. Fill in the missing note values to complete the measures.

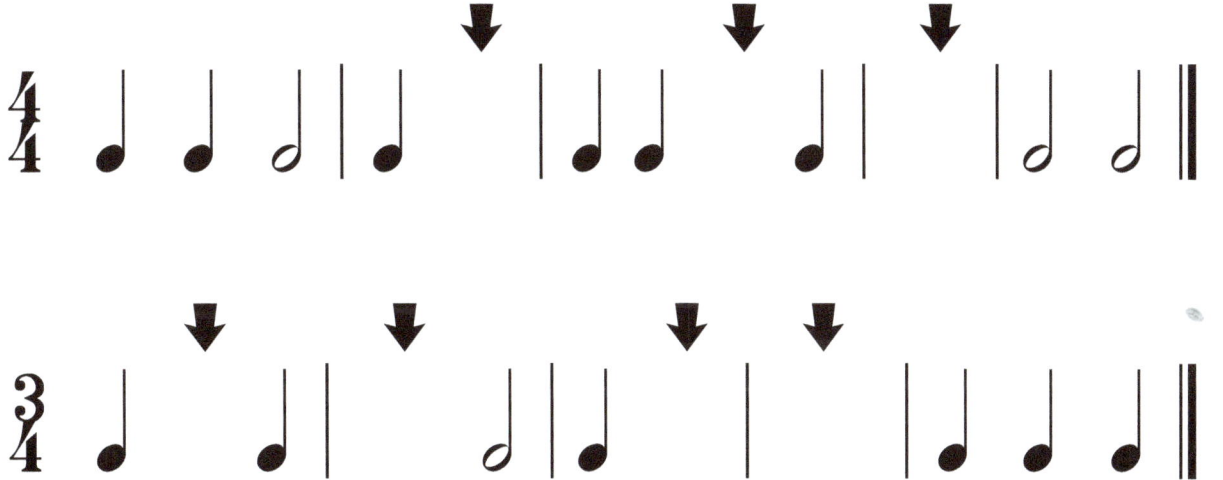

New Ingredients: Rest Values

𝄽 = quarter rest = 1 beat

▬ = half rest = 2 beats

▬ = whole rest = whole measure

→ A whole rest is used for a whole measure in any time signature.

→ Half rests are not used in 2/4 or 3/4 time.

✏️ Practice drawing the new ingredients.

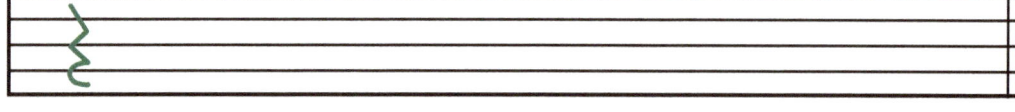

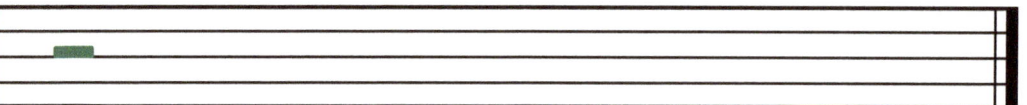

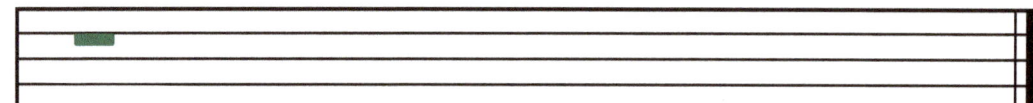

✏️ Circle the matching number of beats for each group of fruit.

   ▬ + 𝄽   ▬ + ▬   ♩ + 𝄽 + 𝅗𝅥.

   ▬ + ♩   𝅗𝅥. + 𝄽 + ♩   𝅗𝅥 + 𝅗𝅥

   ▬   𝄽 + 𝅗𝅥.   𝅗𝅥 + 𝄽

Fill in the missing time signatures for these rhythms.
Practice clapping the rhythms while counting.

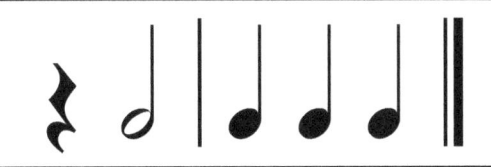
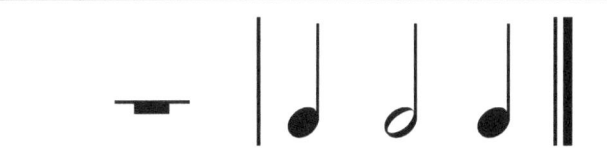

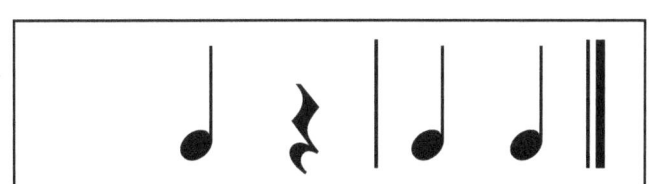

 Fill in the missing notes at each arrow to complete the rhythms.
Practice clapping the rhythms while counting.

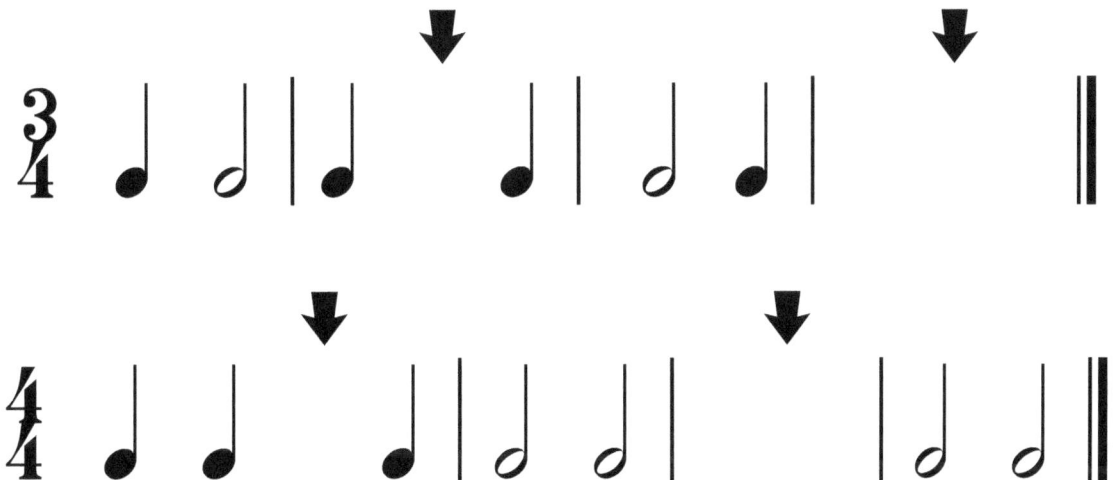

 Fill in the missing rests at each arrow to complete the rhythms.
Practice clapping the rhythms while counting.

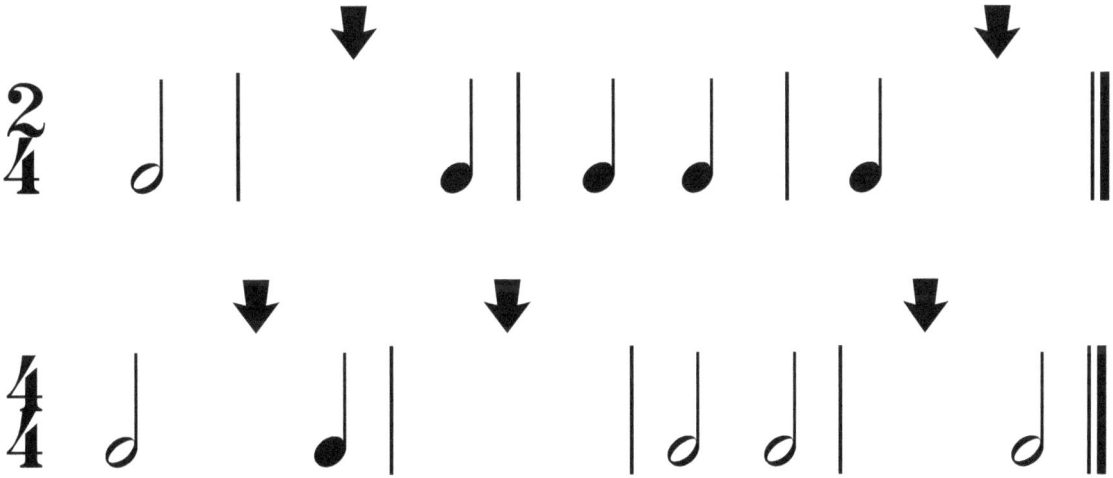

➤ A step can also be called a *second*. ➤ A skip can also be called a *third*.

✏️ Circle either 2nd or 3rd below each of these pairs.

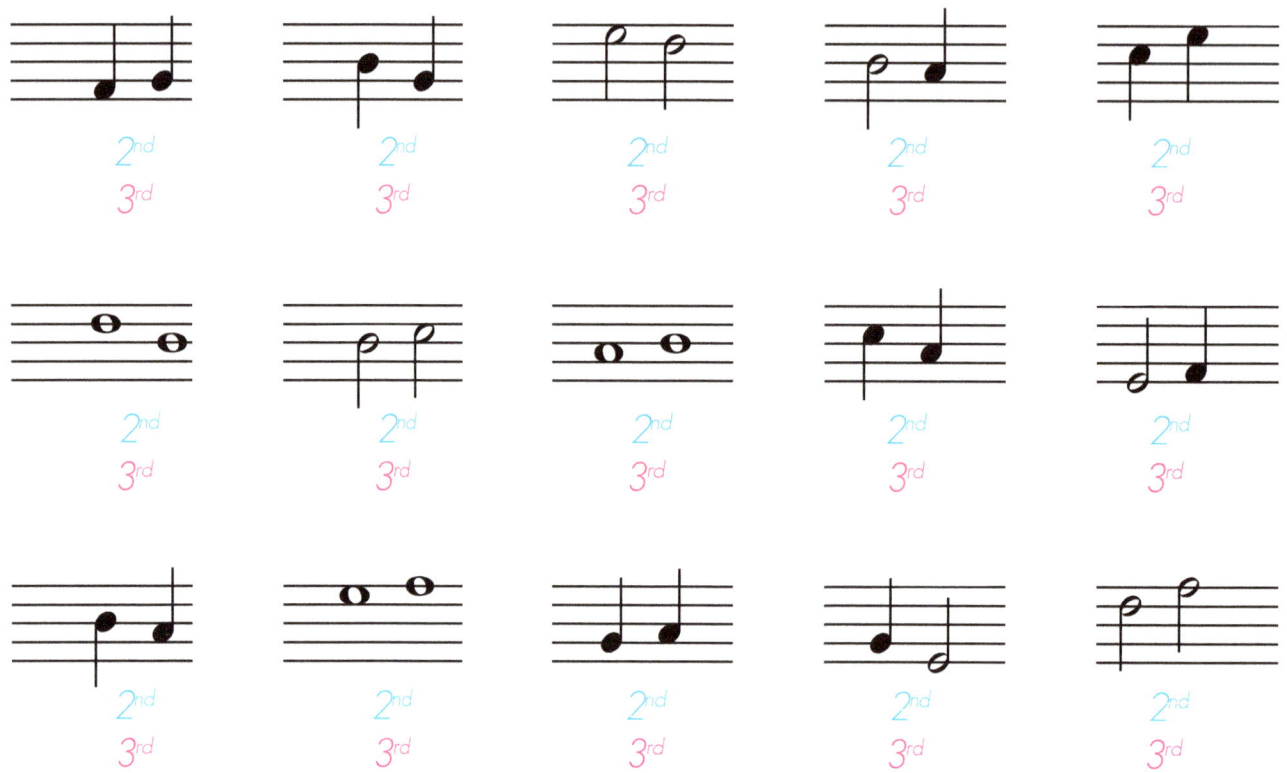

✏️ Draw a note beside the given note to make the intervals.

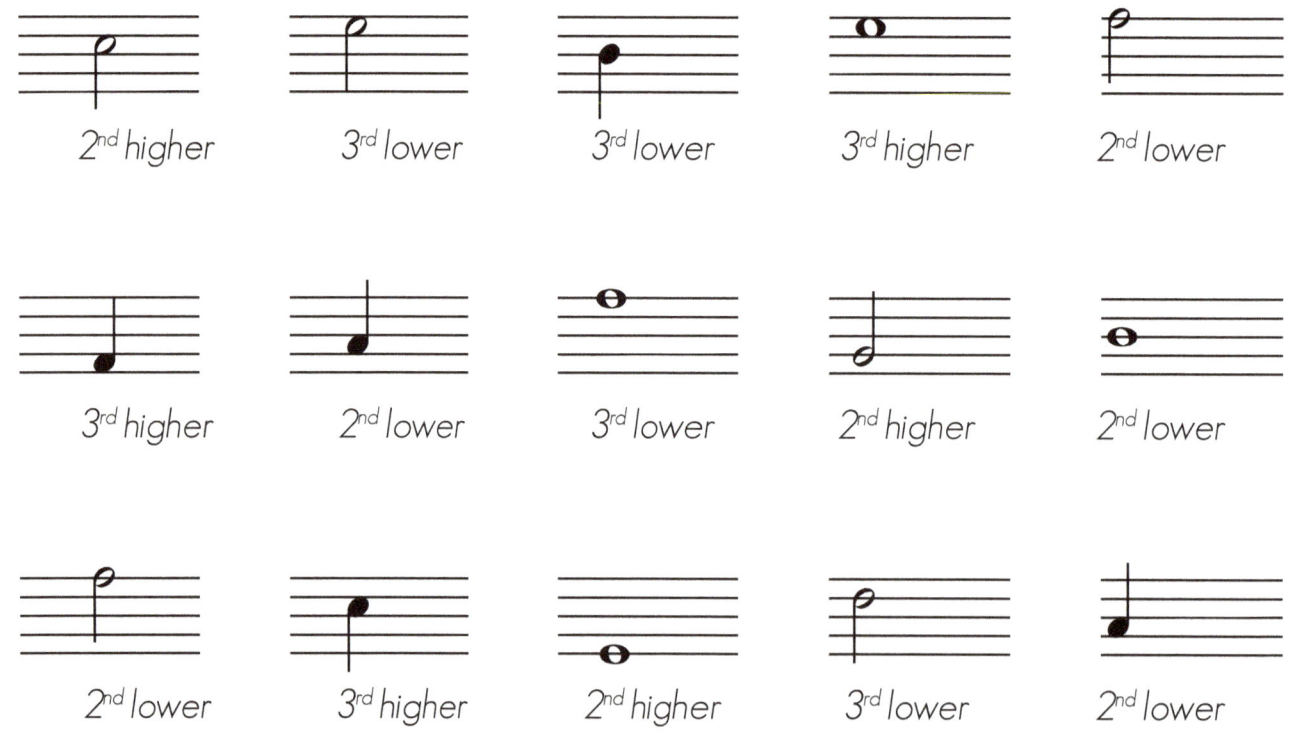

New Ingredients: Solfa
do
re

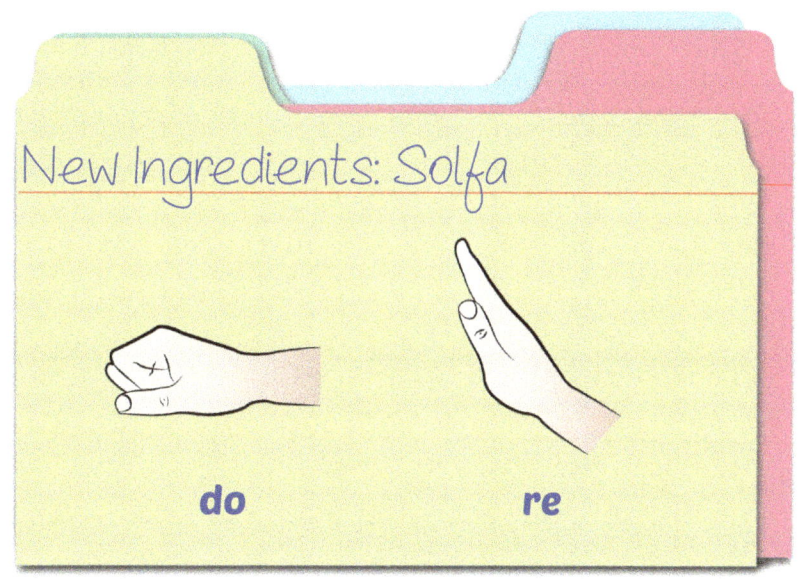

Practice singing the exercises below, using the solfa hand signs. Sing along with the piano at first to help you.

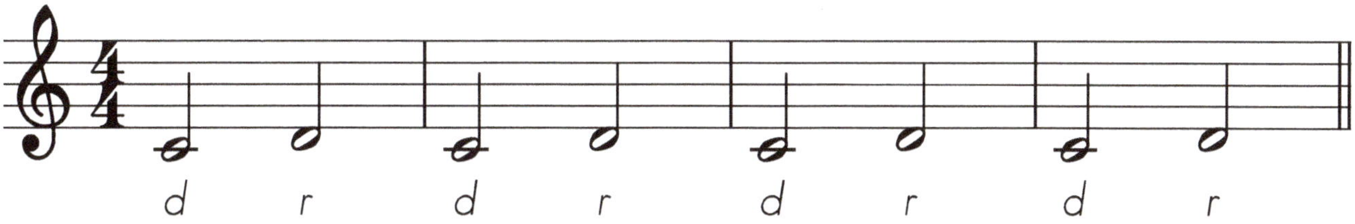
d r d r d r d r

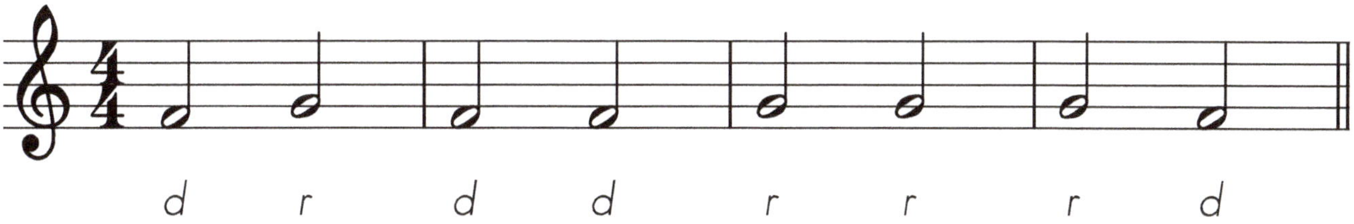
d r d d r r r d

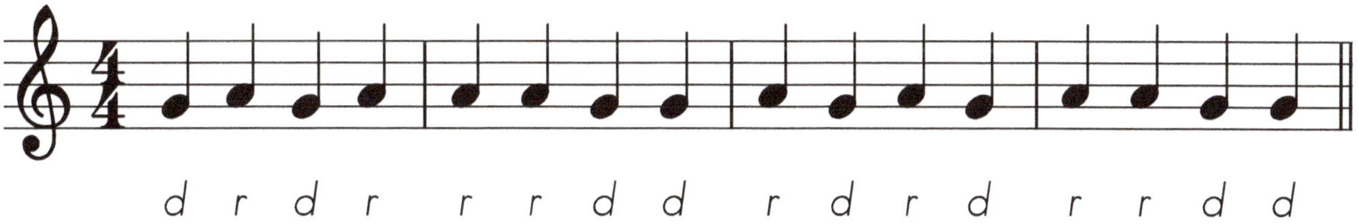
d r d r r r d d r d r d r r d d

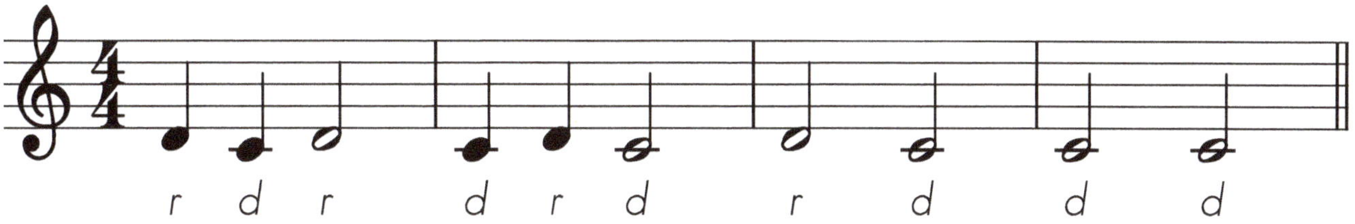
r d r d r d r d d d

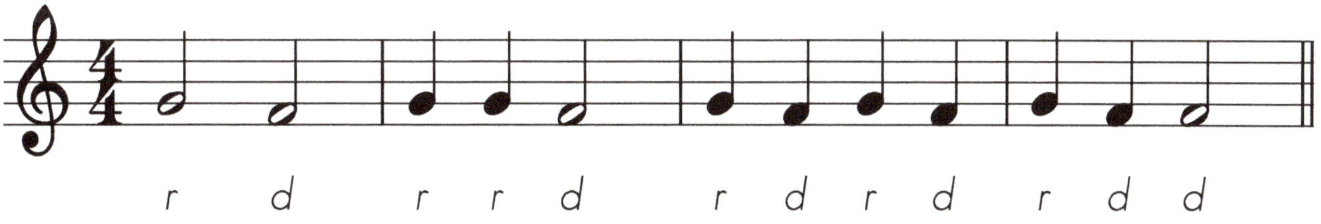
r d r r d r d r d r d d

✏️ Practice drawing the new ingredients.

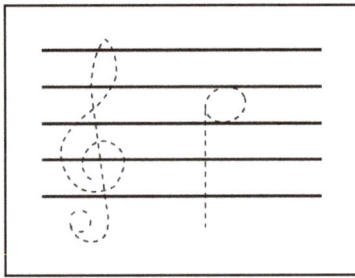 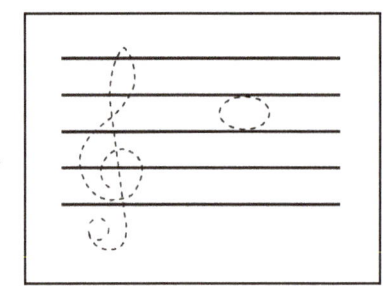 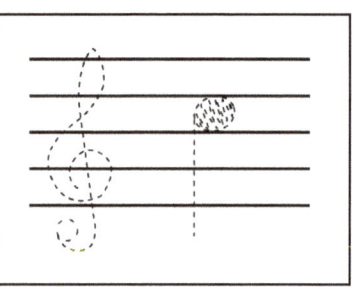

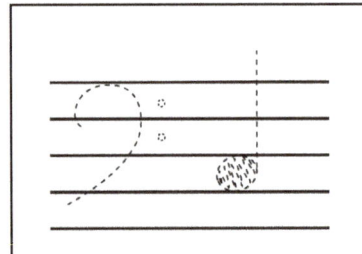 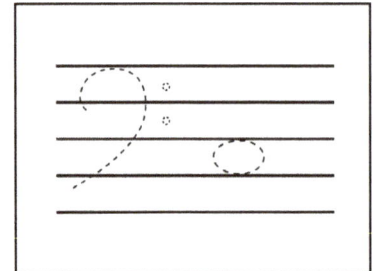 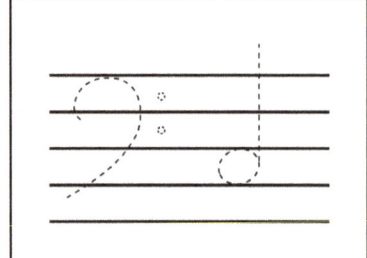

✏️ Circle true or false beside each statement.

Bass F is a space note.	True or False
The second line of the treble clef is a G.	True or False
Treble C is a space note.	True or False
Bass C is a line note.	True or False
Middle C is drawn only in the treble clef.	True or False
Bass F is on the second line down in the bass clef.	True or False
Treble G is a line note.	True or False
Bass C is in the third space up in the bass clef.	True or False

Chapter 3

✏️ Circle the matching fruit for each note.

Level Up!

Get ready for chapter 4 by answering these questions (without looking back through your book!)

1. Write the letter name under each note.

2. Circle 2nd or 3rd below these pairs of notes.

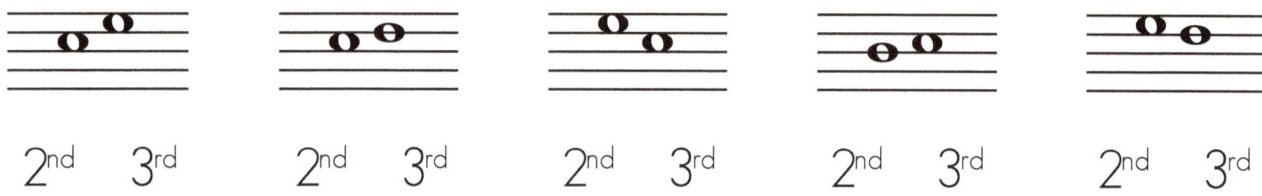

2nd   3rd   2nd   3rd   2nd   3rd   2nd   3rd   2nd   3rd

3. Match the symbol with its full name.

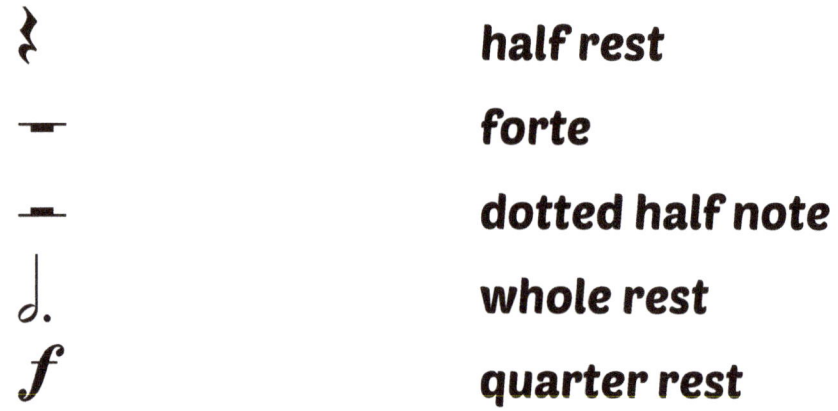

4. Fill in the missing rest values to complete the measures.

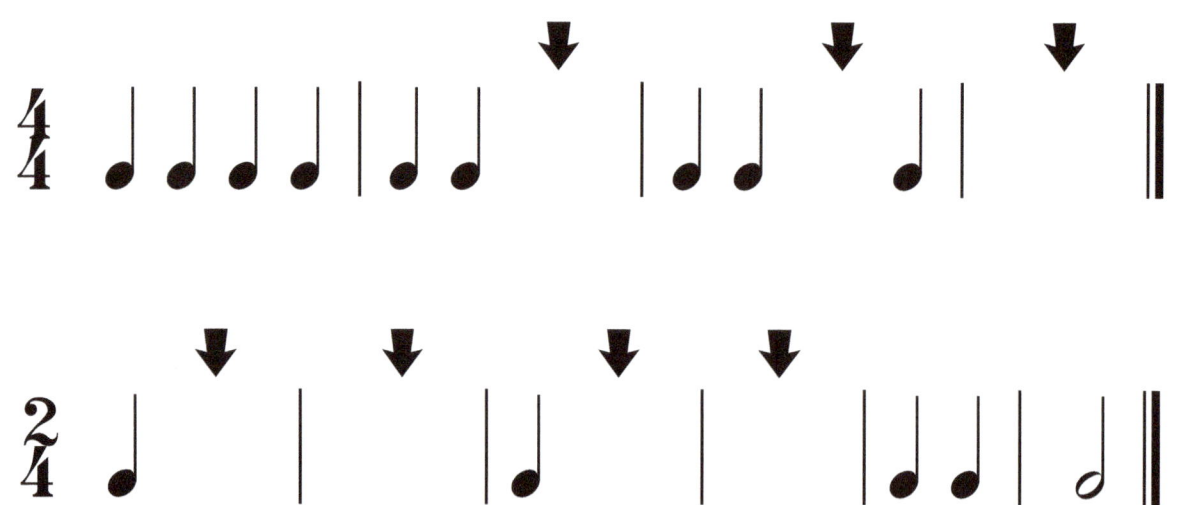

Chapter 4

> ➡ So far we have learned five landmark notes.
> ➡ From these landmarks we can figure out any other note on the staff, by stepping forward or backward in the music alphabet.

 Write the letter name under each note.

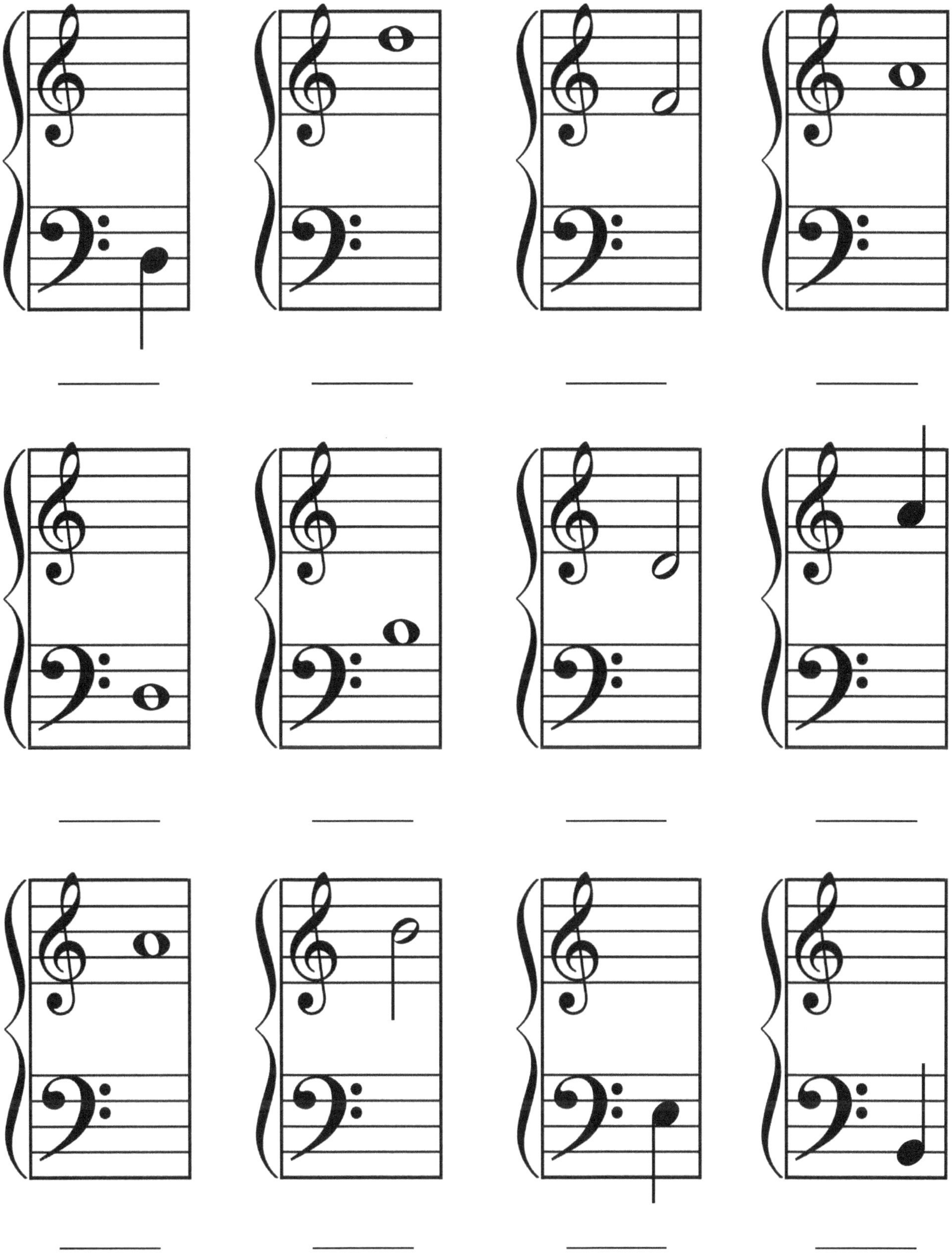

✏️ Color in the keys used in the C major scale.

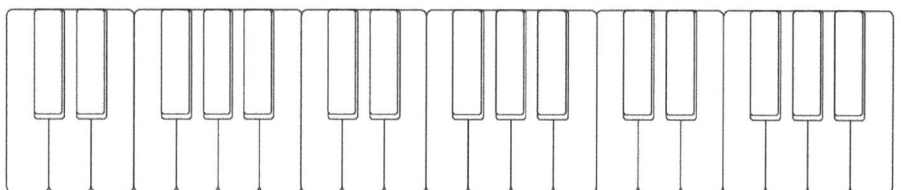

✏️ Trace the...

C major scale, going down, in quarter notes.

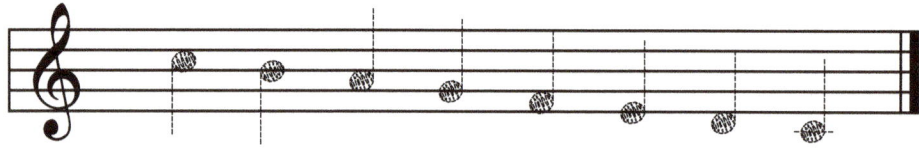

C major scale, going up, in whole notes.

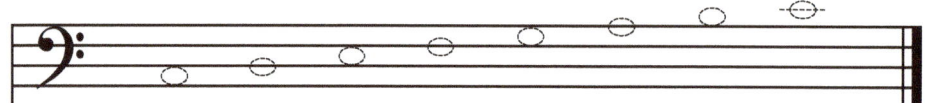

C major scale, going up, in half notes.

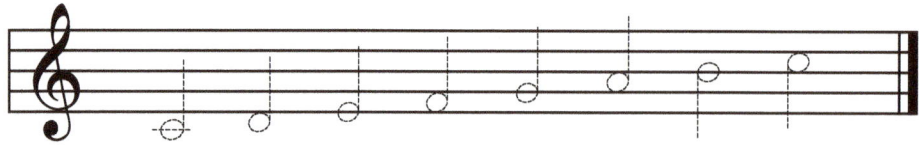

C major scale, going down, in half notes.

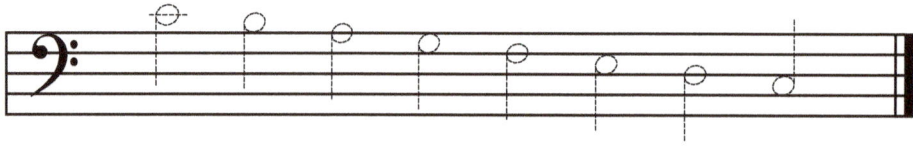

➡ We can figure out notes further away from the landmark notes by skipping forward or backward in the music alphabet.

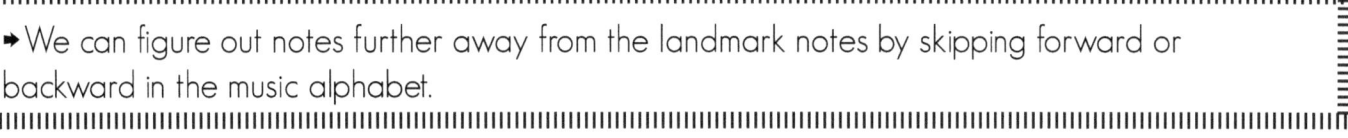

Write the letter name under each note.

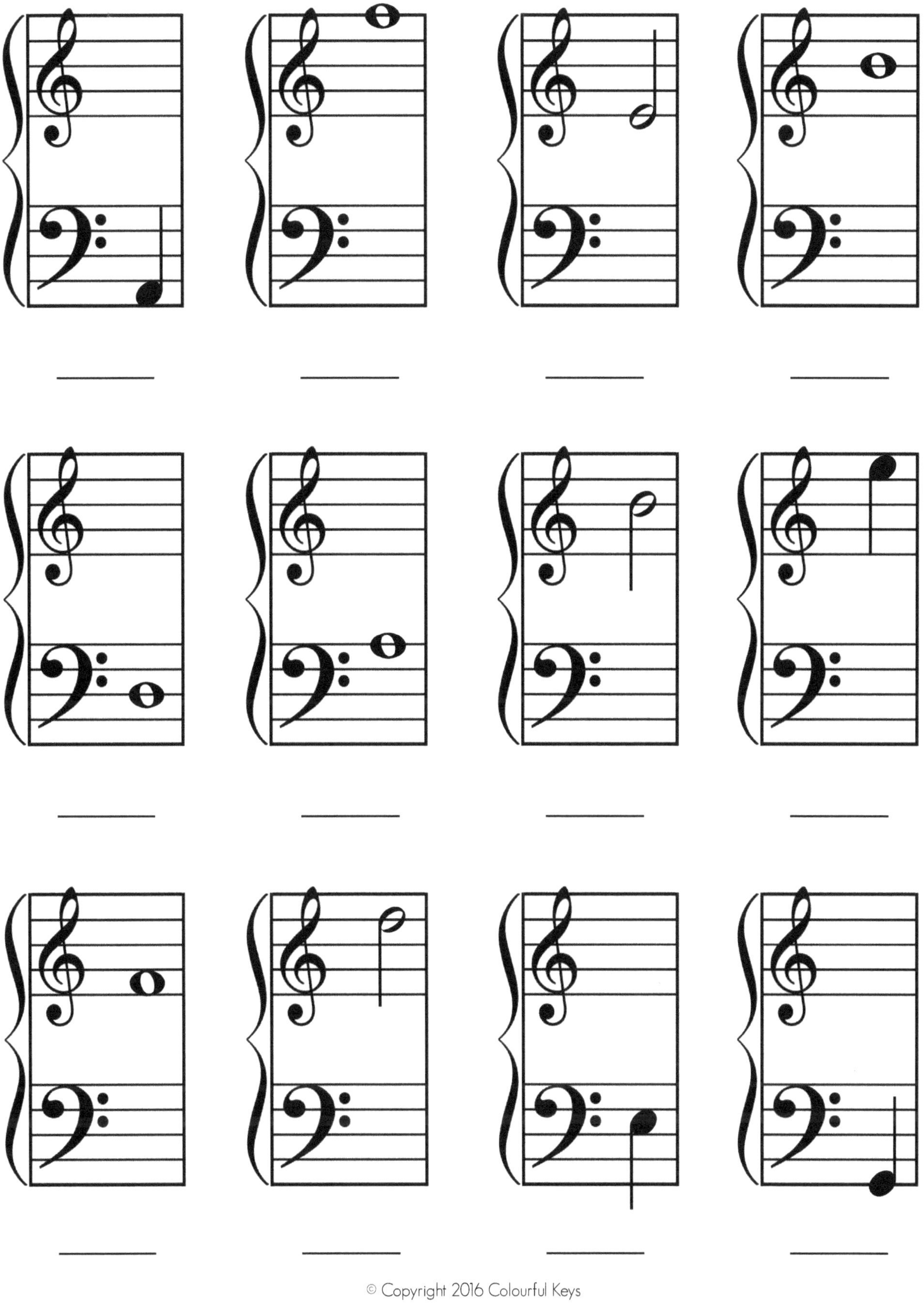

Chapter 4

✏️ Color in the berries as follows:
A = green   B = blue   C = red   D = yellow   E = orange   F = purple   G = brown

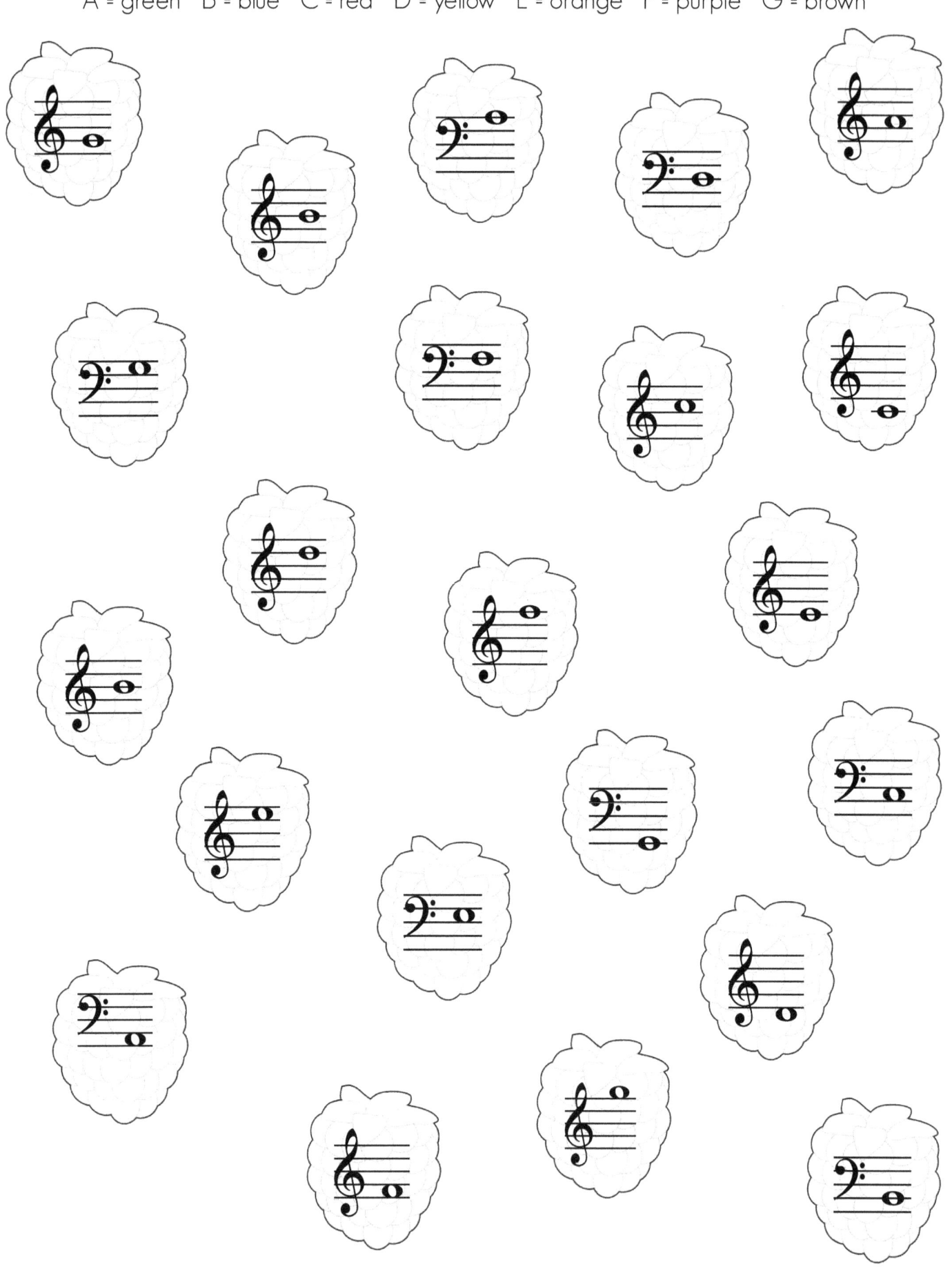

New Ingredients: Solfa

mi

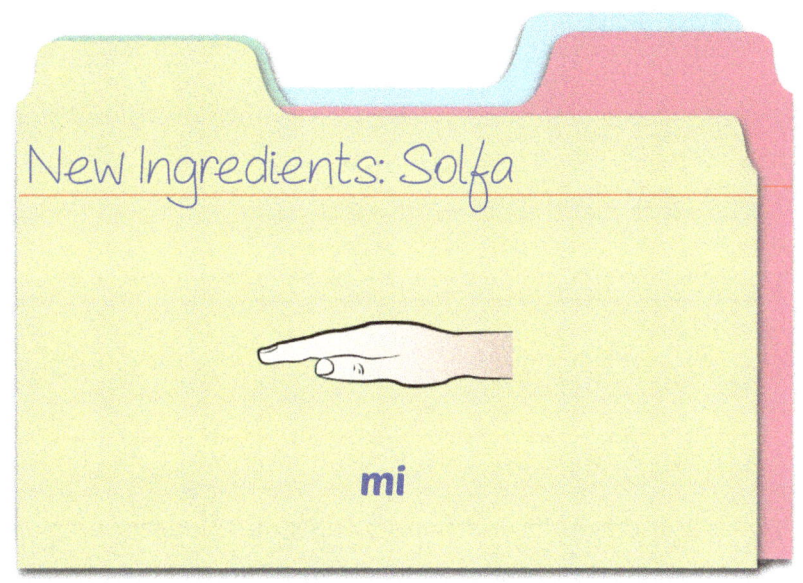

Practice singing the exercises below, using the solfa hand signs. Sing along with the piano at first to help you.

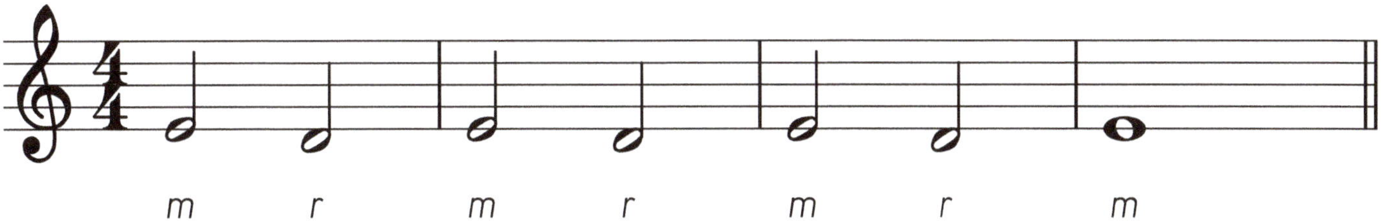
m r m r m r m

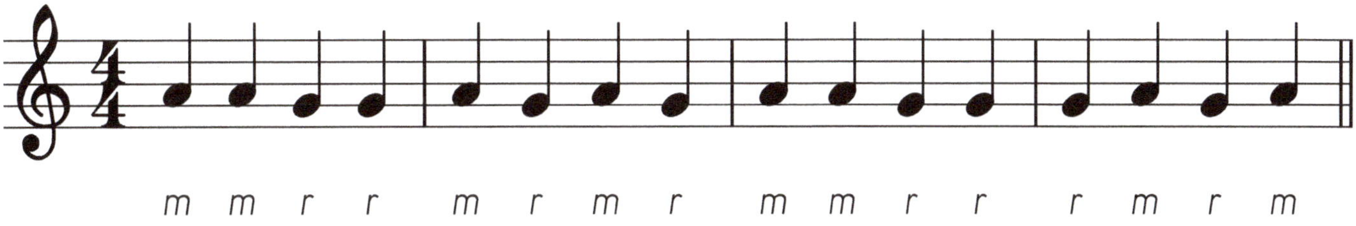
m m r r m r m r m m r r r m r m

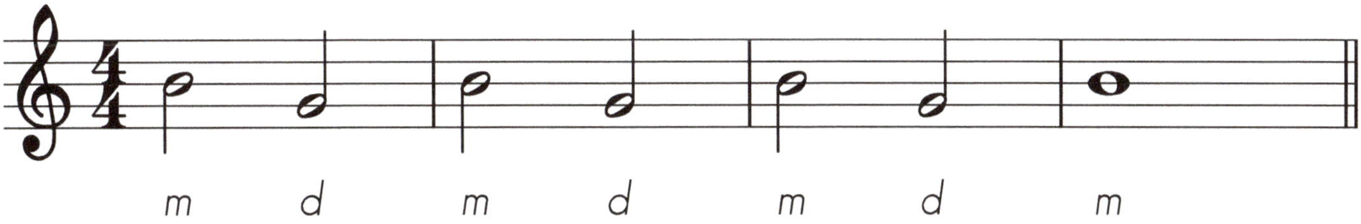
m d m d m d m

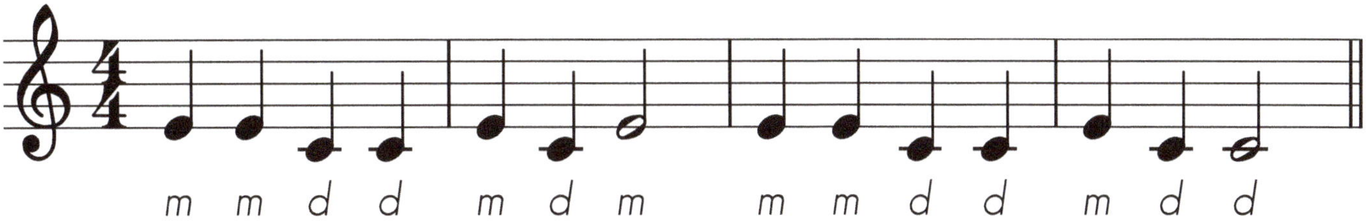
m m d d m d m m m d d m d d

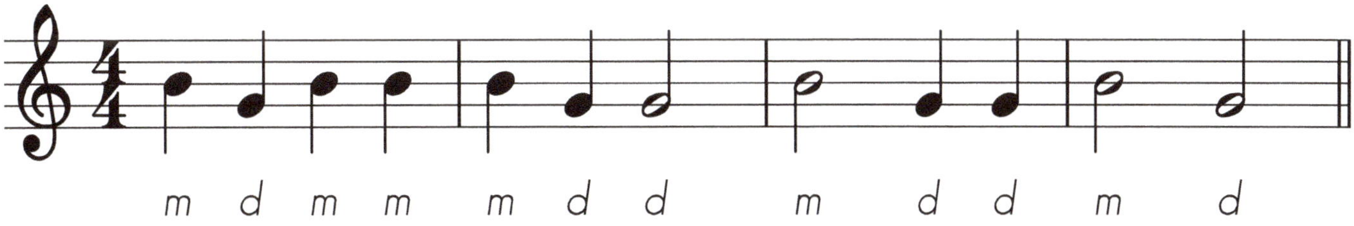
m d m m m d d m d d m d

Chapter 4   Thinking Theory Prep Book

✏️ Match the notes to the correct keys on the keyboard.

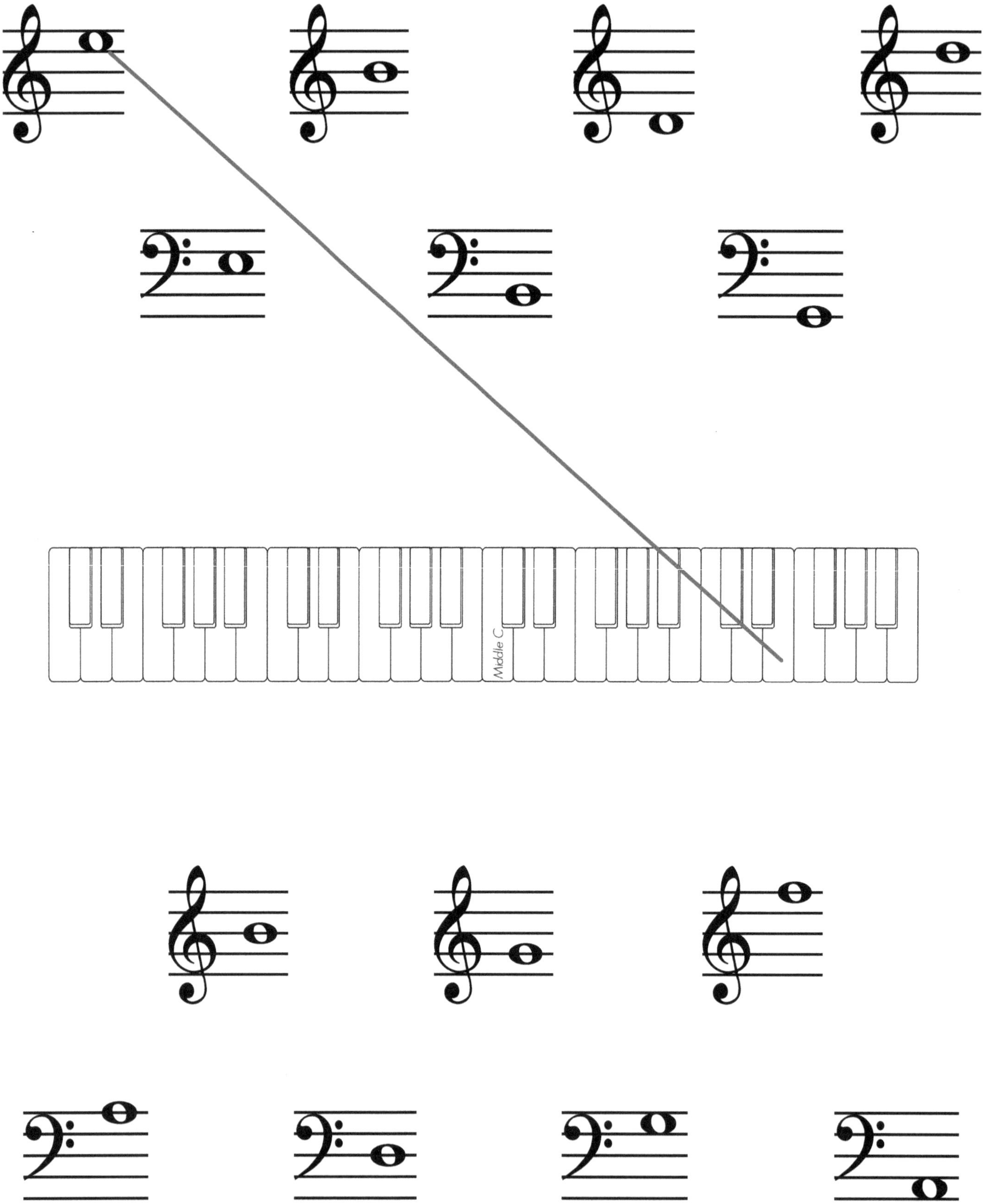

Thinking Theory Prep Book — Chapter 4

Level Up!
Get ready for chapter 5 by answering these questions (without looking back through your book!)

1. Write the letter name under each note.

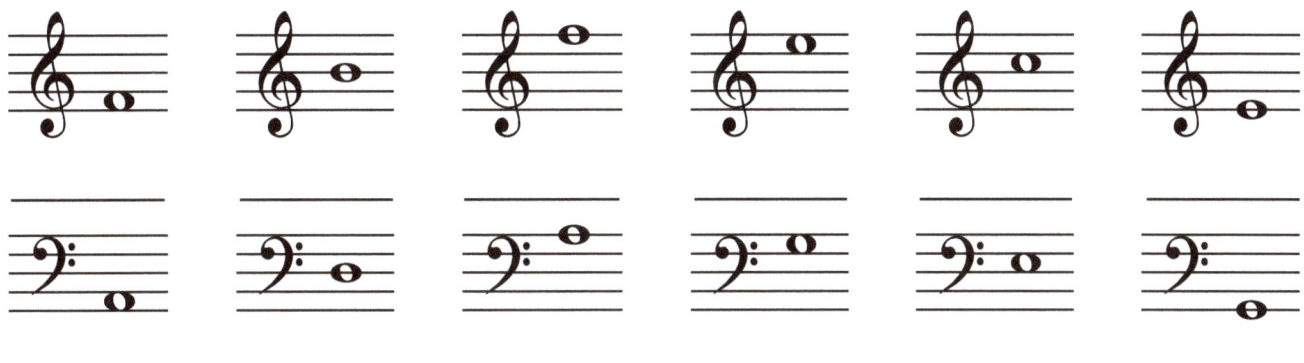

2. Color in the keys used in the C major scale.

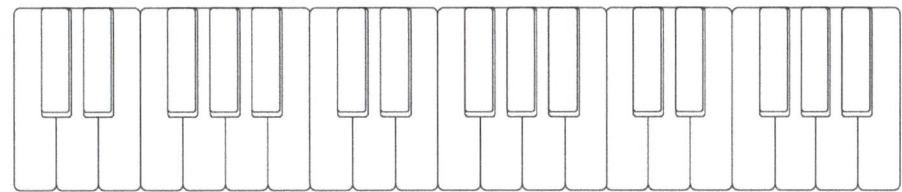

3. Write...

C major scale, going up, in quarter notes.

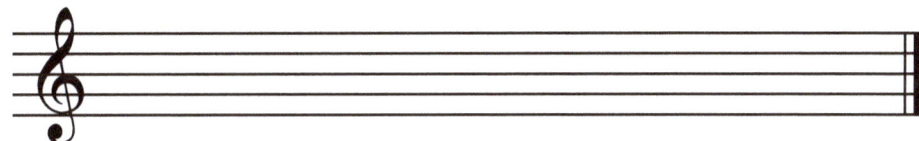

C major scale, going down, in whole notes.

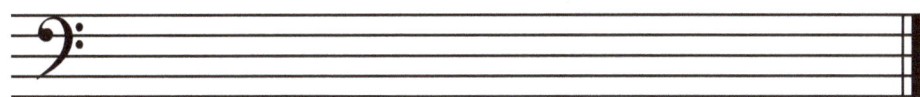

4. How many beats?

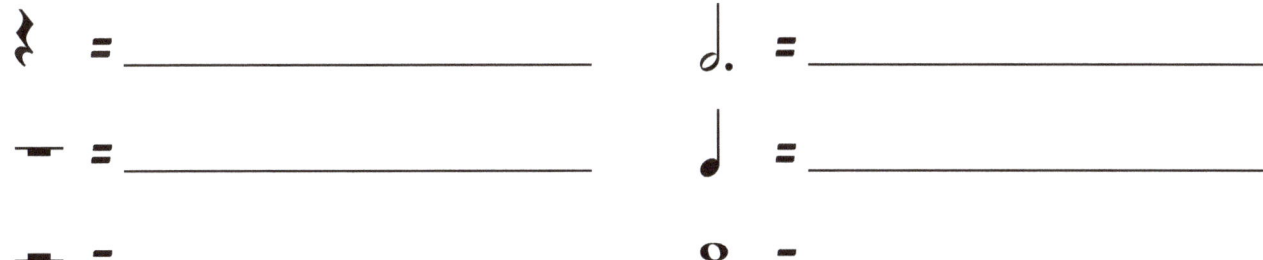

Practice singing the exercises below, using the solfa hand signs. Sing along with the piano at first to help you.

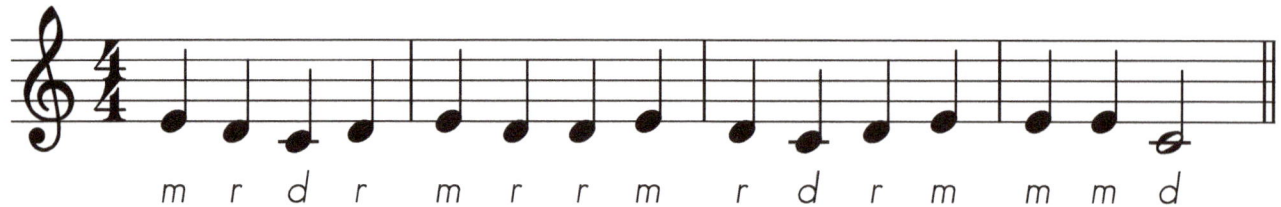

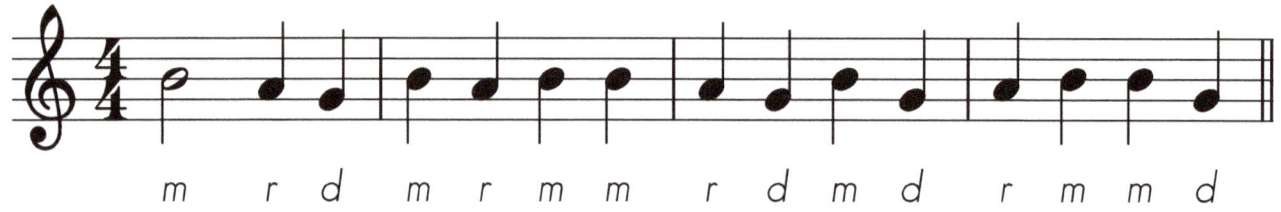

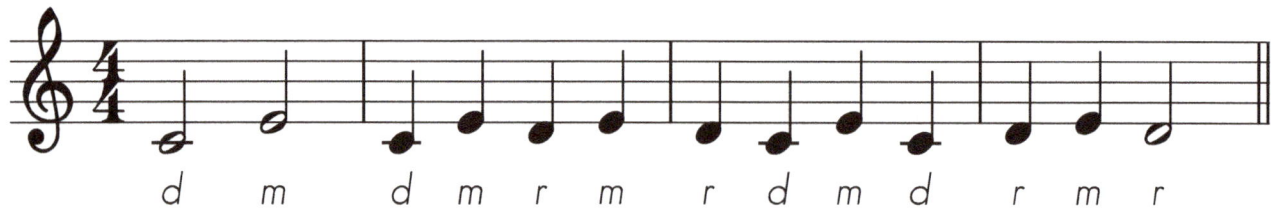

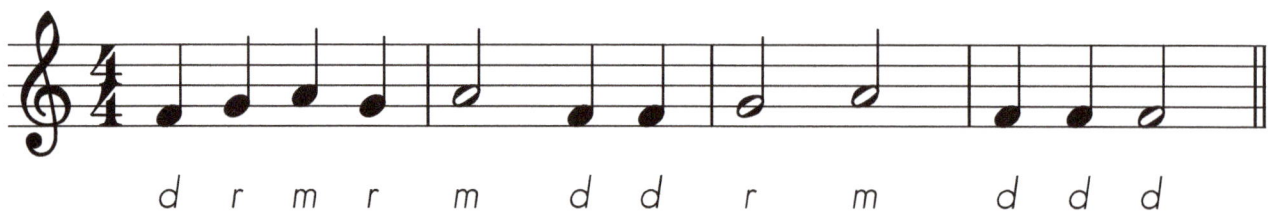

Thinking Theory Prep Book — Chapter 5

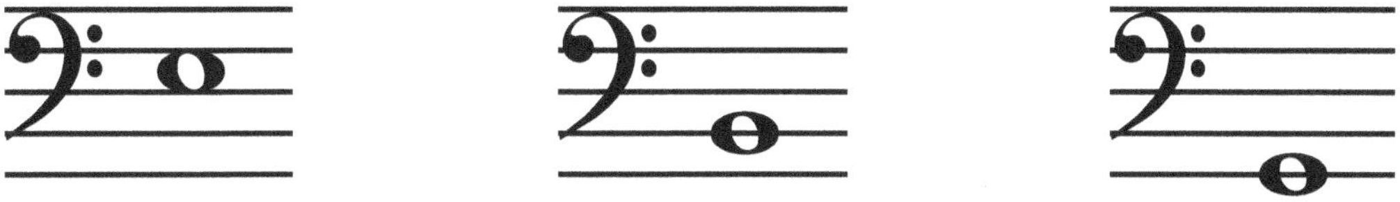

✏️ Draw a note beside the given note to make the intervals.

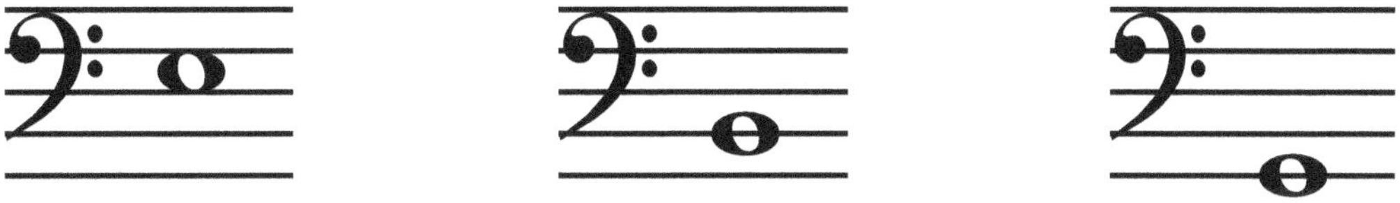

Write the letter names for the notes of the C major scale.

 Color in the keys used in the C major scale.

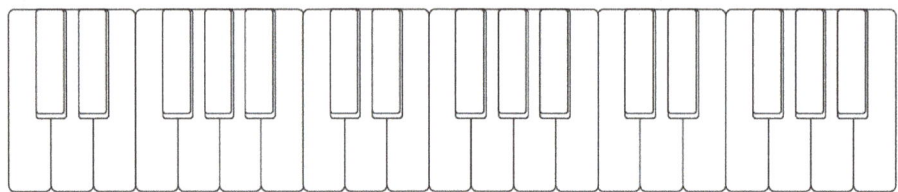

✏️ Write the C major scale going up, in the treble clef.

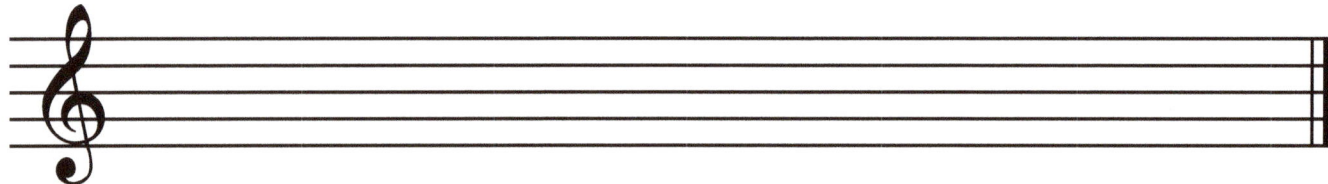

✏️ Write the C major scale going up, in the bass clef.

✏️ Write the C major scale going down, in the treble clef.

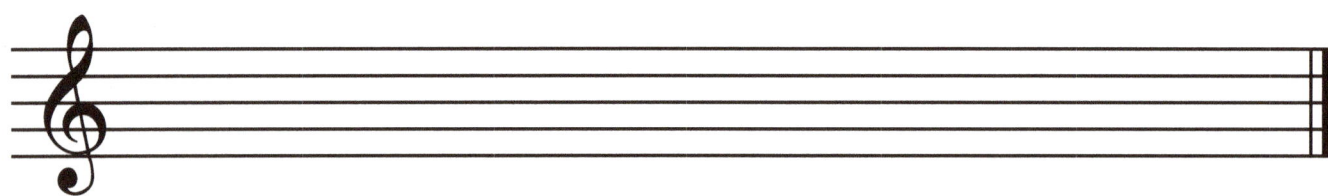

✏️ Write the C major scale going down, in the bass clef.

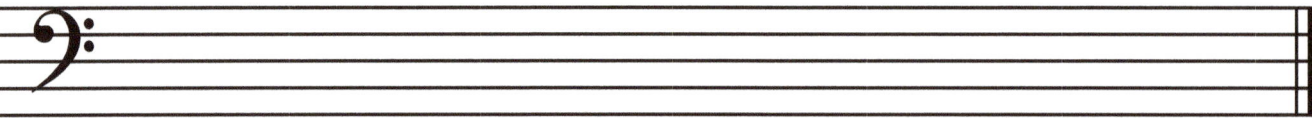

Match the symbol to its name, and the name to the meaning.

Symbol	Name	Meaning
♩	quarter rest	2 beat silence
𝒐	half rest	3 beats
𝒑	whole rest	loud
♩ (half note)	piano	1 beat silence
▬ (whole rest)	forte	4 beats
♩.	dotted half note	1 beat
𝒇	whole note	whole measure silence
▬ (half rest)	quarter note	soft
𝄽	half note	2 beats

✏️ Draw one note to match the value of the notes in each box.

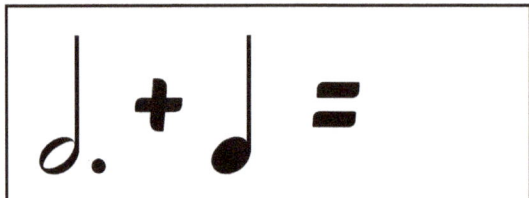
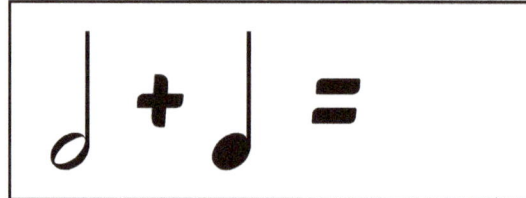
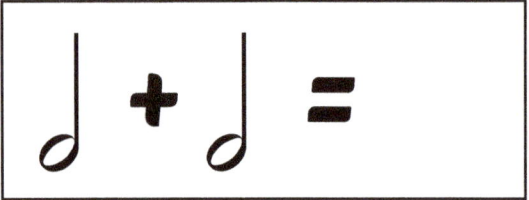
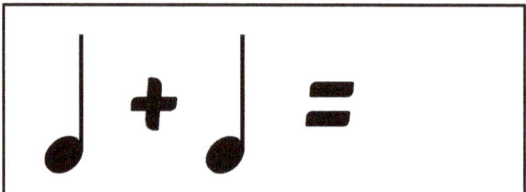

✏️ Fill in the missing notes at each arrow to complete the rhythms.
🖐️ Practice clapping the rhythms while counting.

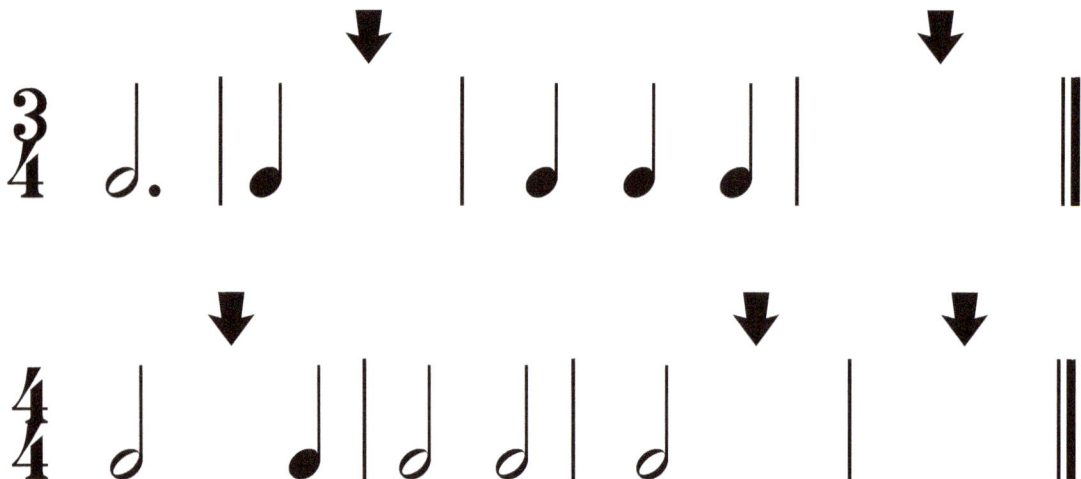

✏️ Fill in the missing rests at each arrow to complete the rhythms.
🖐️ Practice clapping the rhythms while counting.

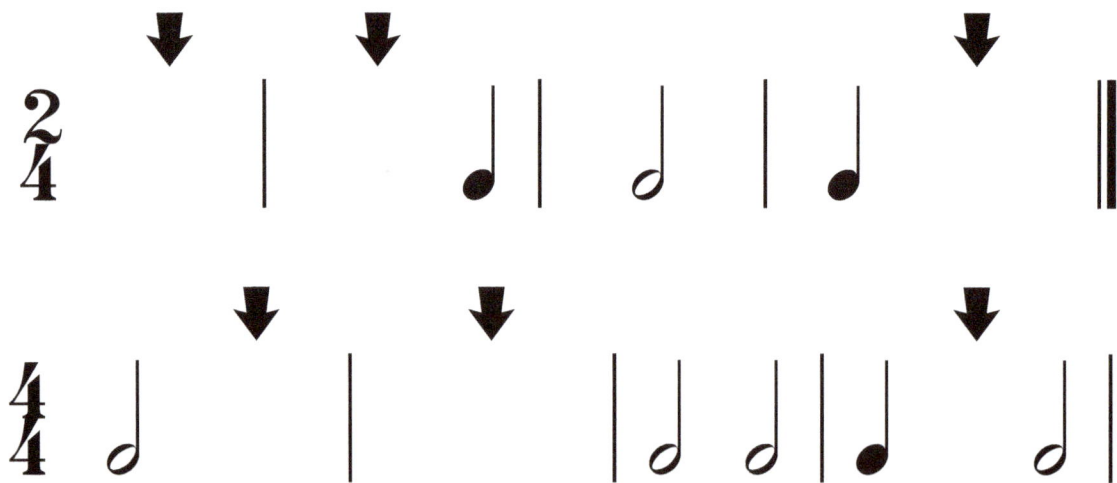

Draw each of these notes on the staff.

 A    G    F    C

 D   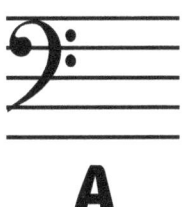 A    F

 B    D    F    E

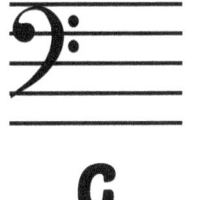 G   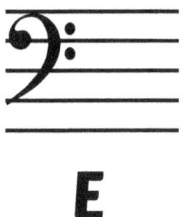 E    B

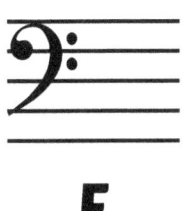 E    A   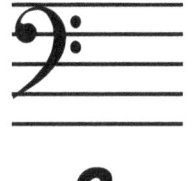 C   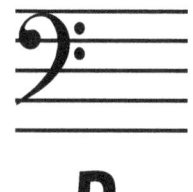 D

 C    G    B

Level Up!
Get ready for chapter 6 by answering these questions (without looking back through your book!)

1. Write the letter name under each note.

2. How many beats? Circle the correct number.

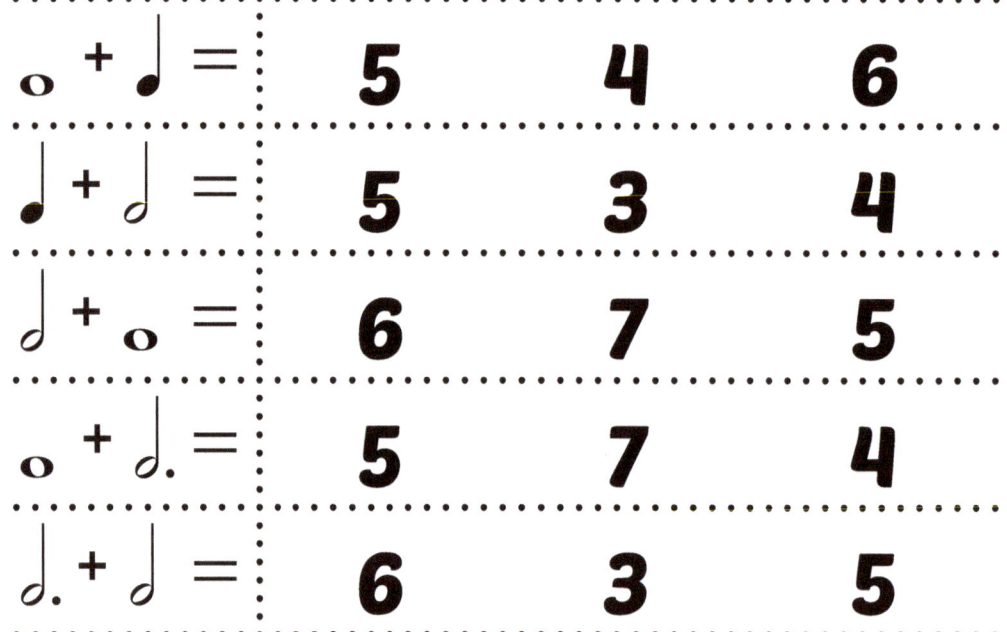

3. Write the...

C major scale, going down, in half notes.

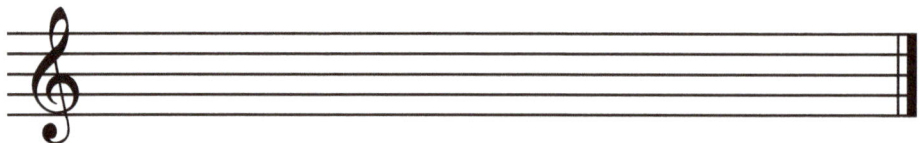

C major scale, going up, in quarter notes.

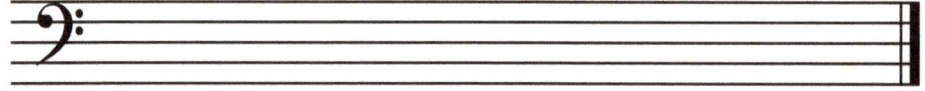

Level Up!

The final test! Answer these questions without looking back through your book!

1. Write the interval under each pair of notes (2nd or 3rd).

    A-C   B-D   D-C   A-G   E-G   F-D   E-D   G-F

    ____   ____   ____   ____   ____   ____   ____   ____

2. Write in the note names under each of these notes.

    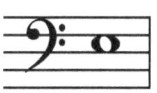 

____   ____   ____   ____   ____   ____

3. Draw notes on the staff for each of these notes.

   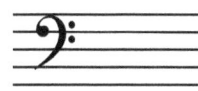 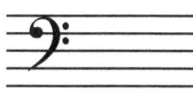 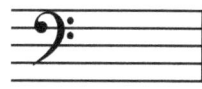

   A   C   F   G   B   D

4. Write the time name and the number of beats for each note or rest.

    ♩ = ___quarter note___ = ___1 beat___

    𝄽 = _____ = _____

    ♩. = _____ = _____

    ▬ = _____ = _____

    ▬ = _____ = _____

    𝅝 = _____ = _____

5. Write the scale of C major, going down, in quarter notes.

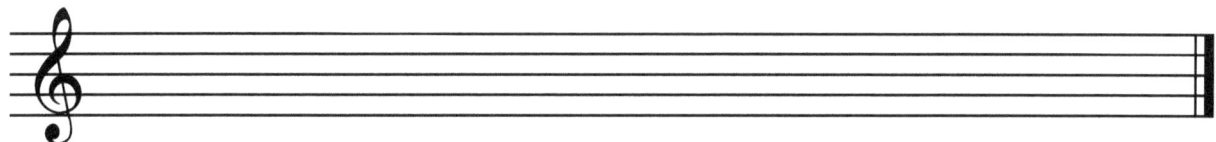

6. Write the scale of C major, going up, in whole notes.

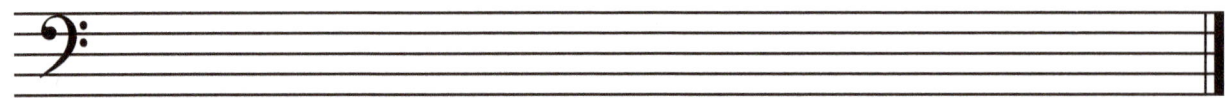

7. Write the interval under each pair of notes (2nd or 3rd).

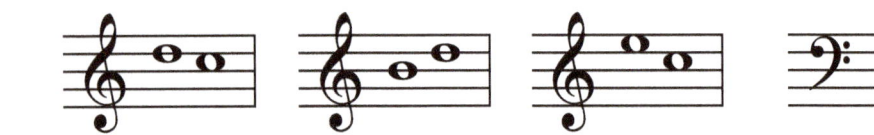 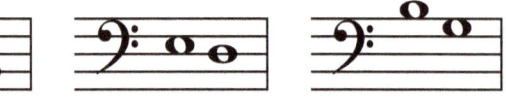

___ ___ ___   ___ ___ ___

8. Write the note name under each highlighted key.

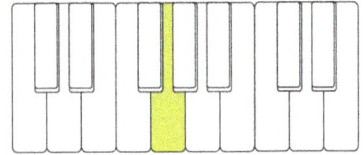   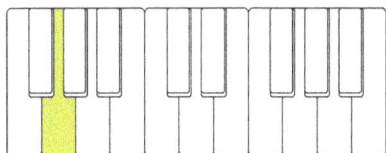   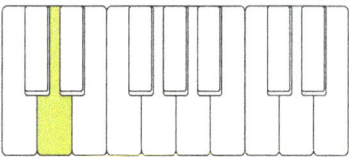

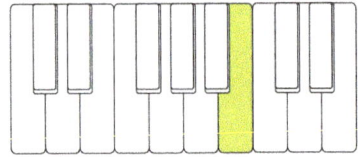   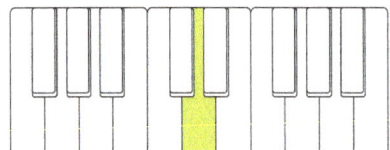   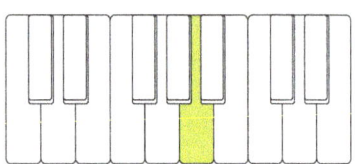

9. Label each hand sign with its solfa name.

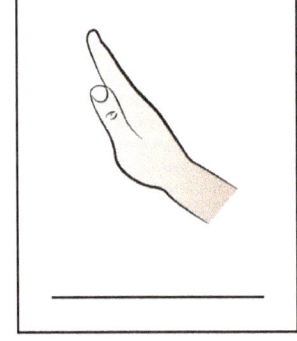   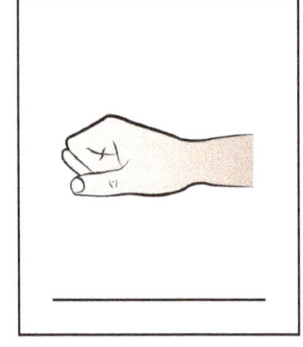   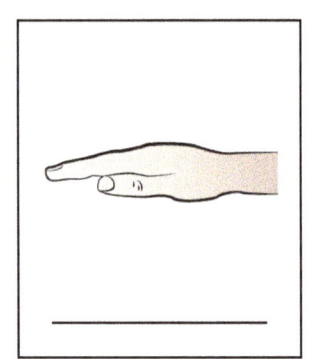

___ ___ ___

10. Add one note at each arrow to complete the measures.

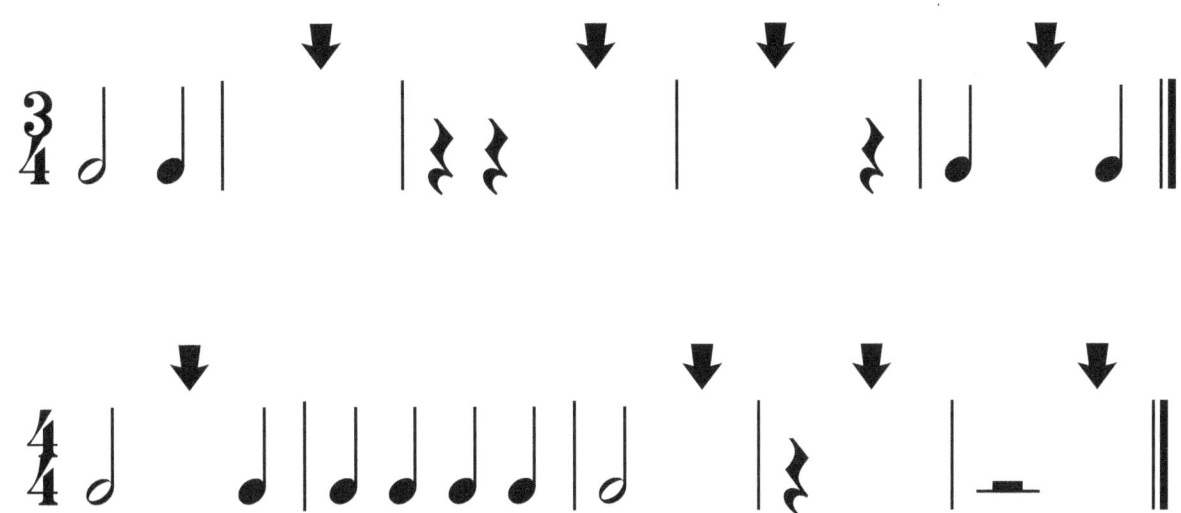

11. Add one rest at each arrow to complete the measures.

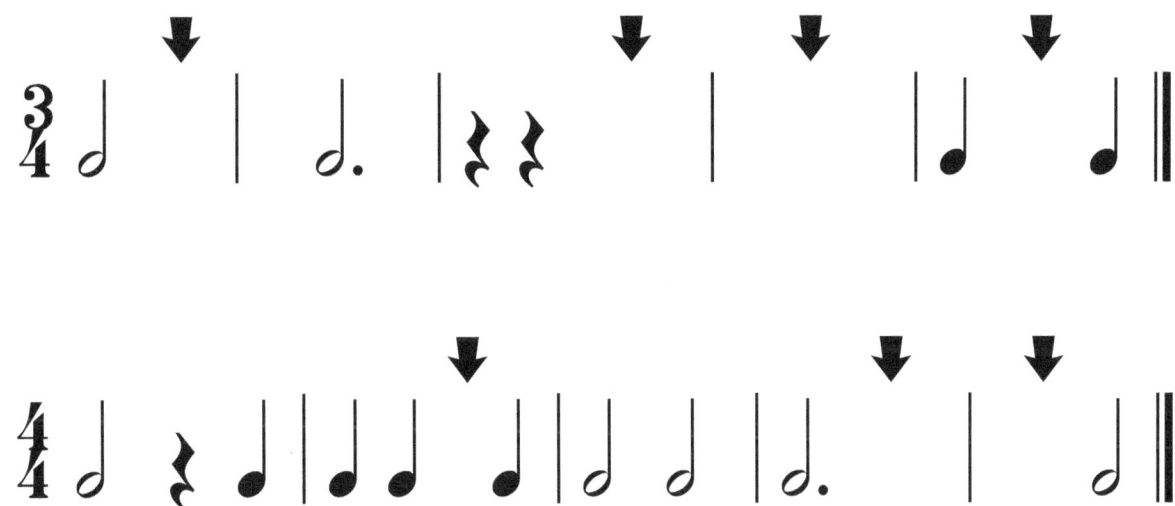

12. Fill in the missing time signatures for these rhythms.

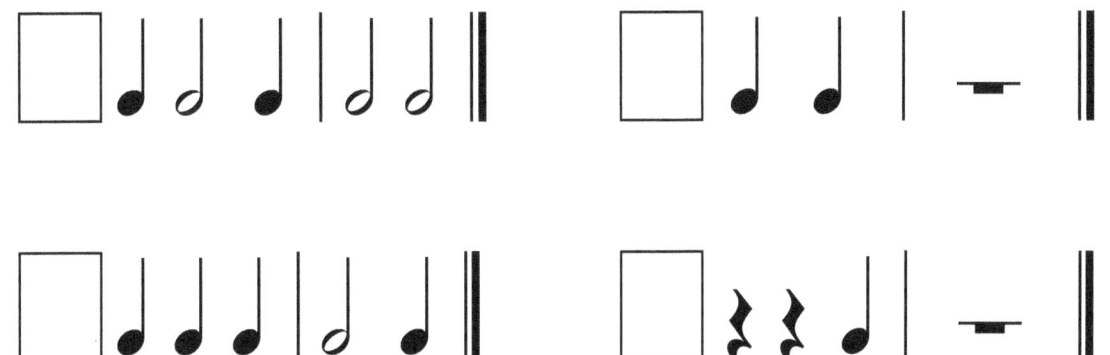

Term Review Cheat Sheet

♩	quarter note	1 beat
♩	half note	2 beats
♩.	dotted half note	3 beats
𝐨	whole note	4 beats
𝄽	quarter rest	1 beat
—	half rest	2 beats
—	whole rest	whole measure
2/4		2 quarter note beats in a measure
3/4		3 quarter note beats in a measure
4/4		4 quarter note beats in a measure
p	piano	soft
f	forte	loud
		F
		E
		B
		C
		A
		D
		G

Where Do We Go From Here?

→ If the student completed this book with ease, and got at least 80% of the final test, you can go straight to Thinking Theory Book One.

→ If the student struggled with this book, and had a lot of incorrect answers on the final test, go to Thinking Theory Prep Book Plus to further reinforce these concepts before moving forward to Book One.

→ If you are unsure which of these routes to take with your student, try using some of the flashcard games with the full set of Thinking Theory Prep Flashcards (available at www.colourfulkeys.ie/thinking-theory), to get a better understanding of where the student is at.

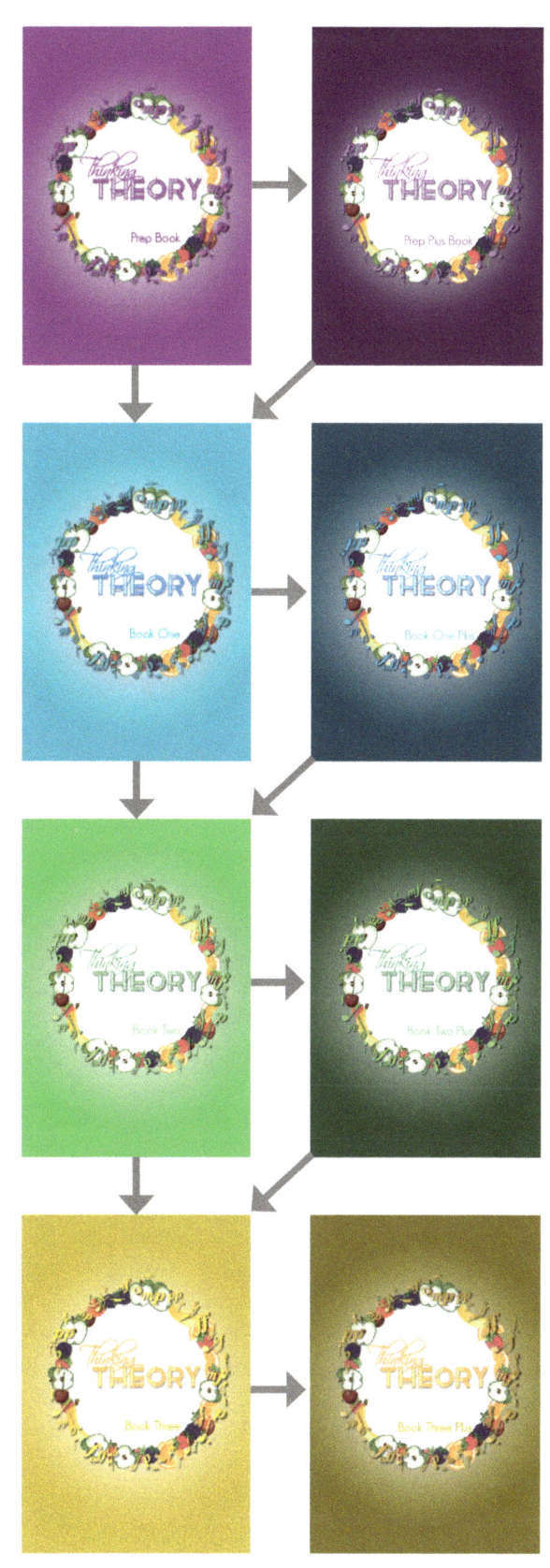

Certificate of Achievement

Congratulations to

_____
(Student Name)

for successfully completing Thinking Theory Prep Book

Date completed: _____

Teacher's signature: _____

www.ingramcontent.com/pod-product-compliance
Lightning Source LLC
Chambersburg PA
CBHW042029100526
44587CB00029B/4346